HOME TO BETHPHAGE

HOME TO
BETHPHAGE

A Biography of Robert Richardson

BY

Cloyd Goodnight

AND

Dwight E. Stevenson

CHRISTIAN BOARD OF PUBLICATION
St. Louis, Missouri

FOREWORD

"OUR literature has thus far had a serious lack," wrote Charles Louis Loos in 1907. "The life of Dr. Robert Richardson has not been written. Dr. Richardson stood in the front rank of those remarkable men, who worked out in their minds a full and correct conception of the religious reformation inaugurated by the Campbells, Walter Scott and others. At an early date Alexander Campbell learned to appreciate the young Dr. Richardson as a man of admirable intellectual qualities, of fine scholarly attainments, an accomplished writer, and one who thoroughly understood, as few did at that time, the real character and aims of the reformation.

"Dr. Richardson's quiet, but nevertheless fruitful life at Bethphage near Bethany, has not given him that fame which a more general public activity would have thrown around his name. But those who knew him well . . . were able to appreciate him at his real worth as an important factor in our reformatory movement." (From an unpublished MS. by F. P. Arthur.)

No man was associated more intimately with the Campbells and with Walter Scott than this unusual doctor of medicine and of letters. He was the pupil of Thomas Campbell and of Walter Scott, as well as the latter's convert, coeditor, and bosom friend. He was the Campbells' family physician. As coeditor of the *Millennial Harbinger,* he was the confidant and adviser to its distinguished senior editor from the year 1836, often carrying the entire editorial burden and the heavy correspondence of that publication. It was his fertile brain which originated some of the most striking ideas to which Alexander Campbell later gave currency. His writings are second in volume only to those of Campbell himself.

When Bethany College came into being, it was with Robert Richardson as a member of its first faculty and board of trustees. Often, when the president was on tour, it was "R.R." who became acting president. He was involved in the educational beginnings of Hiram College and he served as vice-president of Kentucky University. His luminous writings were the earliest and clearest interpretation of the principles of the Disciple movement. As Campbell's biographer, he wrote the monumental *Memoirs of Alexander Campbell*, an important source book of Disciple history which must lie at the foundation of every other biographical effort.

Perhaps the principal reason why Robert Richardson has not become a celebrated figure long before this is that he was not a public speaker. Quiet, unassuming, and retiring, he was content to draw to himself little public notice. It was his wish and his genius to lose himself in the great cause of reform. It has been our serious loss that in this self-abnegation he almost succeeded.

After a visit to Bethany, June 16, 1869, Editor J. F. Rowe, of the *American Christian Review*, informed his readers:

> Beyond the musical waters of the purling Buffalo, and over the broad brow of that gigantic hill, is located the arcadian retreat of Prof. R. Richardson, author of the *Memoirs of Alexander Campbell*, and who, in his silent, and unobtrusive rural home, is about completing the second volume of that splendid work so

eagerly sought after by all the admirers of the great reformer. Who shall write the life of Prof. Richardson? for he too is a mighty man. [*Millennial Harbinger*, 1869, p. 409.]

Mr. Rowe's question has had to wait eighty years for an answer. The late Cloyd Goodnight, distinguished president of Bethany College, worked long to supply it. He devoted his spare hours over a period of fifteen years to that end. When he was cut off at the very peak of his effectiveness at the age of fifty in 1932, he left behind him the first rough draft of his unfinished manuscript. The chief treasure of this draft, which was nearly 400 pages long, was a faithful transcript of a large body of Robert Richardson's private correspondence and some of the doctor's daybook.

It was at first my hope that I could edit this manuscript and offer it for publication largely as it was; but a careful reading soon disclosed its unfinished condition and made it clear that much was still to be done. Plainly, President Goodnight had intended to revise, rearrange, and rewrite the entire *Life*, for he was far from ready to send the book to press. The only thing for me to do in that case was to immerse myself in research, reading everything ever written by or about Richardson, and then using all my sources, including Dr. Goodnight's manuscript, to write the biography from the beginning in my own way. That is what I have done.

My admiration for Dr. Goodnight, who was my teacher and my own college "Prexy," as well as my debt of gratitude to him, are very great. This book is designed to complete a phase of his lifework which he was not allowed to finish for himself.

There are charm, deep wisdom, gentle goodness, mystic faith, and authentic greatness in the life of Robert Richardson. To convey its story to you is a sacred privilege. We hope and expect that Richardson's beloved Bethphage, with its flowering gardens, its neat and bounteous fields, its large happy family, and its quiet, book-lined study will become to you, as it was to him, a precious haven of recaptured peace and renewing faith. For myself, born as I was almost exactly one hundred years later than he, I can say that a century has been no barrier to one of the most meaningful friendships I have ever formed.

DWIGHT E. STEVENSON.

Lexington, Kentucky
November, 1948.

ACKNOWLEDGMENTS

As is always true of a book requiring much research, the authors have been dependent on personal assistance generously given from many quarters. This help has been both extensive and various. We regret that it is not possible to acknowledge its specific character in each instance, but among those to whom we are chiefly indebted, I should list the following: Charles Henry Ambler, Virginia Ashbaugh, E. Hugh Behymer, George W. Bennett, T. Hassel Bowen, Lin D. Cartwright, Garnett Dean, Rose Demorest, Thelma Dodge, Enos E. Dowling, N. W. Evans, F. P. Farmer, Winfred E. Garrison, Irvin T. Green, W. H. Hanna, Roemol Henry, William B. Kennedy, F. D. Kershner, Robert E. Kleesattel, Elizabeth Meek, R. H. Miller, James DeForrest Murch, Mrs. Margaret Neal, C. D. Pantle, Charles Penrose, Rhoda Perry, Mrs. Ada Pilchard, Mr. and Mrs. Charles Rayl, Claude E. Spencer, Agnes L. Starrett, Paul Stauffer, Jr., Paul H. Stevenson, Virginia Stevenson, Dwight Ward Stevenson, Harriet Thomas, Bradford Tye, Dean E. Walker, B. R. Weimer, Mrs. R. H. Wynne, and Eva Jean Wrather. In addition, three of the late daughters of Robert Richardson— Mary B. Chapline, Fannie R. Thompson, and Emma R. Wharton—contributed valuable papers and personal accounts. The grandchildren and great-grandchildren of Dr. Richardson have helped enthusiastically and in large measure; from among them I would mention Mrs. Margaretta Armstrong, Virginia Freeman, Charles A. Lambie, Jr., N. R. Howard, Encell C. Richardson, George C. Richardson, and Nathaniel Robert Richardson.

ACKNOWLEDGMENTS

In particular, I wish to mention President W. H. Cramblet, of Bethany College, who first suggested the publication of the work and who has shown a keen interest during its writing and given substantial support in the issuance of the book to the public. Mrs. Cloyd Goodnight, widow of the coauthor, has been most encouraging and cooperative at every turn. I am also indebted to my colleague, Dr. Howard Elmo Short, professor of church history, who read the entire manuscript and suggested several clarifying revisions. Burton Johnson, book editor, whose patient hours spent on any book always far exceed the call of duty, has rendered many services; among these none is more important than a suggested rearrangement of the opening chapters which has greatly increased the interest of the story.

My wife, DeLoris, has devoted unnumbered hours to the role of an unpaid research assistant and typist. Without her help it is doubtful whether the book would have been written, and certainly if it had been written it would have been a much poorer volume.

D. E. S.

CONTENTS

CHAPTER I

NOT PEACE BUT A SWORD

HIS medical calls over for the day and the last patient gone, young Dr. Robert Richardson sat at his desk re-reading a well-fingered letter, which had come five days before. How should he answer it? His emotions were so mixed up. On the one hand, there was the sustaining elation that had been with him ever since he had followed Walter Scott to the Western Reserve for his baptism. On the other, there was his vexation over the complete misunderstanding of his father. "Misunderstanding" was hardly the word for it—the *rage* of his father! He had, too, an immense respect for the author of this letter. Although he knew the missive by heart, he read it yet again, his mind fumbling meanwhile for the right words with which to reply. It was dated at Pittsburgh—

JULY 9th, 1829

MY DEAR YOUNG FRIEND,—You will not, I trust, take it amiss if I express to you the surprize and regret with which I heard from your father, of the change in your religious sentiments. But my design in troubling you with this, is not a controversial one. I merely wish to set before your excellent judgment a few reasons for questioning the propriety of your course, even supposing that your conclusion were a right one.

You are the eldest of a numerous family; I believe I may add, the best endowed both by nature and by education, and engaged in a highly respectable profession. That you should be looked up to in a great degree by your brothers and sisters, and peculiarly cherished by your parents, is, under these circumstances, a very rational consequence. That you are so, is a fact with which you must be perfectly acquainted.

His eyes trailed on down the page. How these words misjudged him! Because he had failed to consult his parents over this recent change in religion, he was charged with contempt for their opinion. He had done nothing "to prepare them for the change" or "to lighten the blow." In short, his action was unfilial and cruel. This was a masterful attack upon Robert's weakest point. He continued to read:

Have you done as you would, one day, wish your son to do by you? . . . Have you not been led by your zeal to do a positive evil, at least in the mode pursued to secure your object? And are you sure that your course has produced to others the hundredth part of the pleasure, that it has inflicted pain, on those whose love for you is probably greater than that of the whole united world besides?

In spite of the vigor of his attack, the rector was writing without hostility. He really wanted to be helpful, but it was a helpfulness that could not rise beyond the limits of a mild and rather urbane religion. The young doctor read on.

I trust you will pardon the frankness of this expostulation. I am a father, and therefore may presume that I can estimate the misery of a parent who sees and mourns over the estrangement of a darling son, much more correctly than you can *yet* do. God grant that you may never experience the terrible reality of such a visitation. But beholding, as I did, the grief of your father; hearing him say that he had passed a sleepless and a wretched night in consequence of your conduct in this matter, and observing the tears of strong emotion which his manhood could not restrain while he spoke, I could easily conjecture the state of your mother's mind, and thought it a duty to intrude myself no longer as pastor, but as a christian friend, to ask you whether you are not bound in conscience and in principle, to acknowledge your error in taking such a step without consulting them?

Well, since receiving this letter, he had certainly done all he knew how to do to bring about the reconciliation which it counseled. From his understanding mother there had been immediate and wholehearted capitulation. But from his father? Nothing but wounded pride and cold, uncommunicative anger. Unrelenting, unforgiving anger. An anger that seemed to say, "You are disinherited from my affection forever!"

Robert's eyes returned to the rector's letter:

I do not mean at all to impeach the soundness of your religious views. My sincere desire is to have you unmolested and entirely free, even from any unwelcome solicitation on that subject. But I do beseech you not to suffer this breach between you and your parents to remain unclosed for want of a speedy and thorough effort to heal it. In the mode of your procedure, you have been exceedingly to blame, because this mode was a plain declaration of want of confidence, want of kindness, want of reverence, want of filial submission. I confine myself to this single point, believing it a plain one, and in the hope that, however your light may exceed mine in the other doctrines of christianity, we shall agree in the practical application of the moral law: "Honor your father and your mother, that your days may be long in the land which the Lord your God gives you."[1]

The signature was that of John Henry Hopkins, rector of the Episcopal church of Pittsburgh.

The young doctor laid the letter aside and reached for quill and paper to frame his reply. To place religion within the confines of family loyalty and to make its claims subservient to the expediences of respectability, even when the appeal was expressed as urbanely as Hopkins' letter had phrased it, astounded him. He had recently discovered how searching and unconditional the call of faith really was, how far above old loyalties, and how wholly other from respectability and expediency. He had hoped that a decision so crucial would find acceptance in his own family; but if not, there was little question as to where his first loyalty belonged. Had not his former rector read his New Testament? "Think not that I am come to bring peace to the earth. I came not to bring peace, but a sword. For I am come to cause dissension between father and son, between mother and daughter, between mother-in-law and daughter-in-law; so that a man's enemies will be found in his own family. He who loves father or mother more than me, is not worthy of me."[2]

He dated his reply at Carnegie, Pennsylvania—

JULY 15th, 1829

MY DEAR FRIEND,—As it would be highly inconsistent with my profession to take amiss any friendly attempt to convince me of a supposed error, I am very far from doing so in regard to that which you have made. On the contrary, I have to thank you for endeavoring to convince me that I was at fault in not consulting my parents upon my choice of religion, although my own heart as yet acquits me. As I cannot, however, exonerate myself from the charge before others, without declaring the motives which prompted me to that choice, it becomes necessary for me to offer to you an apology for preferring Christianity to Episcopalianism. An apology for becoming a Christian!—and to a professed minister of the gospel! This is strange—but circumstances require it!

He then set out to show Mr. Hopkins how he had already let his father do too much of his religious thinking for him, and that he had only lately come to stand on his own spiritual feet. "I was born and bred an Episcopalian," he observed. "At least as soon as I knew my right hand from my left, I found myself an Episcopalian — . . . as far as compulsory attendance on Episcopalian ceremonies could constitute me one, and lived, until my sixteenth year, without religion and without God in the world."

Alluding to the religious instruction of a former teacher, Walter Scott, though not calling him by name, he went on to say, "About this time a beloved Christian brother (not an Episcopalian) directed my thoughts and affections, in some degree, toward the Lord Jesus, as the Rose of Sharon that had no thorn; and the occasional reading of the scriptures, and a more particular attention to prayer and to sermons was the consequence." This teacher had never urged him to receive baptism or to leave the Episcopal church, "though he had ample opportunity to do so." At any rate, the young correspondent wrote, he had not left the Episcopalians at that time, but instead had finally offered himself for confirmation in that church. He reminded Mr. Hopkins that this step had been taken at his father's and the rector's request, even though there had been some prompting of a genuinely spiritual nature. "No motive," he declared, "had so strong an influence over my conduct in this matter, as the fear of disobeying my earthly parent."

The experience of confirmation, however, had not brought peace to his soul, he told his former rector. In fact, the burden of sin seemed to grow heavier; and all his efforts to rid himself of it were in vain. Following this was a period which he described as being "compounded of long seasons of torpid religious despondency," alternating with "transient glimpses of the happiness which religion would have afforded" if it had been possessed "in its purity."

At some length, he went on to express to Mr. Hopkins the growing disillusionment he had experienced as he observed the sectarianism and petty strife within the denominations with which he was familiar, declaring that this had been an important factor in leading him to embrace a religious movement which he conceived to be more in line with the principles laid down in the Holy Scriptures.

Believing that my Heavenly Father meant what he said, and that in everything essential to salvation his words were plain, I threw behind me all sectarianism, and took up the bible. And I took it up with the resolution that what I discovered to be my Father's will, I would endeavor to perform: and if the idea of consulting any human being about the propriety of doing what I believed to be the command of God, had ever entered my thoughts, it would have done so only to be discarded as a suggestion of Satan.

Considering the Christian church as it was first formed by the Apostles, and the ancient gospel as preached by Peter on the day of Pentecost, I perceived that faith in Jesus, as the Son of God and Saviour of sinners, was the first duty; the second, repentance;

and the third, baptism for the remission of sins and the gift of the Holy Spirit; and the fourth, that we should walk in newness of life.

He then told Mr. Hopkins how he had studied his Greek Bible, only to come to the conclusion that scriptural baptism was always and solely by immersion. Having reached this conclusion, he had acted at once, and his action had been between himself and his God.

Writing these words, the young physician's mind raced back to the three days he had spent on horseback searching out Walter Scott on the Western Reserve. He recalled how he had found him at Shalersville, and how he had surprised his former teacher with his sudden appearance, and then astounded and delighted him by his request for baptism. So he had become one of "the Reforming Baptists"; a "Campbellite" some would call him. And there was irony in that situation, too, for two of those with whom he was now associated had been his former teachers, employed by his own father and entertained under his own family roof in Pittsburgh. At that time, of course, his father had not known or cared about the religious views of Thomas Campbell and Walter Scott. It was enough for him that they were accomplished scholars and excellent teachers. Curious, now that Robert thought of it, that they had never told him anything of the work of reform they were doing in the church! Curious, too, that he had come to their way of thinking without suspecting that his change in sentiments would throw him with the Campbells! Of course, he had known that it would bring him into association with Scott.

He returned to the writing of his letter. His study had led him to the action which Hopkins so deeply deplored. So be it. "I could not conceive that I was bound, by any principle, to consult my parents, or anybody else, about the propriety of fulfilling this duty," he now wrote. "Besides this, my father's 'feelings and principles' in religion, which you say, are worthy of 'sacred regard,' I knew to be strictly and exclusively Episcopalian, . . . and I feared to rouse in my father those violent passions which it seems Episcopalianism has no power to subdue."

That Nathaniel Richardson was now taking such a vital interest in his son's religious life was a matter of some surprise to him, Robert continued. "Religion never was the subject of conversation between me and my father, and I never perceived him to be interested in it. . . . As long as I 'went to church' as the phrase is, all was well. My being a christian seemed to be a secondary consideration, or rather no consideration at all. I know not how he could expect me to consult him in a matter in which I never saw him interested, and about which he never conversed with me."

He bade Mr. Hopkins imagine how displeased his father would have been if he had consulted him and afterward had gone against his express wishes! That fury would have been a storm indeed! Moreover, there was something very peculiar here: "I am happy; but my father is angry. And this is strange—that he should mourne for me—that my joy has become his sorrow, and my happiness his displeasure."

He went on to explain that his action was in no sense to be taken as a mark of ingratitude or disrespect toward his parents. Conceiving his first duty to be to God, he said: "My affection for my parents is unabated. . . . To my earthly parents my obedience in things not interfering with rights of conscience, and abundant gratitude is due; since they labored for my comfort in temporal things, and incurred expense, and bestowed opportunities of education on me, more than I deserved or duty required of them."

It had been Mr. Hopkins' conjecture, expressed by letter, that Robert's mother must have been even more offended and hurt than his father. This was an unfounded conclusion, Robert now explained. "You seem to think that my mother regrets my happiness more than my father. You are in error. She rejoices in it. One presents the picture of 'Affection conquered by Pride'; the other, 'Pride conquered by affection.'"

His zeal for his new religious commitment returning to the foreground, he went on.

Finally, lest any thing I have said should cause the church of Christ to be misrepresented, I will observe, that for many years, in different parts of Europe, a few of the sheep of Christ, in various sects, have recognized their Master's voice, and refused to listen to the voice of a stranger: from some congregations, two or three—from others, eight or ten, separated themselves, and resolved to take the scriptures as their guide. All these appear to have fallen on the same plan, without any knowledge of each other, i.e., the plan formed by the Apostles. And this 'wild fire,' as you like to call it (in contradistinction, I suppose, to the glimmering taper of Episcopacy), is now making its way in America.

He concluded his letter with an appeal, almost evangelistic in note:

That the purity and simplicity of the ancient gospel may cease to be foolishness to men, and that the elected by God may be enabled to walk worthy of their high vocation, is my prayer to him who is able and willing to save all who come to him through Christ our Lord.

He sealed the letter and prepared it for the post. In the days that followed, when no reply came, and when nothing had availed to heal the breach between himself and his father, he felt himself engulfed in loneliness. His medical practice was busy enough, and his neighbors and patients were friendly enough; but still he was lonely.

It was out of that loneliness that he sent off a letter to Walter Scott, urging him to visit western Pennsylvania and try his evangelistic powers there. Perhaps his success in winning thousands of converts on the Western Reserve would be repeated here, and—who could tell?—his whole family might see the light, and his troubles vanish! "I long to see you!" he pleaded.

Scott, replying under date of July 28, 1829, sought to undergird the young convert's courage:

If the Religion of Jesus is worth a straw it is worth the Universe. . . . I bless God for your conversion and may God bless you and make you a blessing to many people.

You long to see me? I also long to see you exceedingly. I want most assuredly to reap the whitening Harvest in your parts but we must be prudent; the time of natural harvest is not always that of the Spiritual. This season is not quite opportune for the assault which I purpose making on the distracted profession of your country. . . .

My best respects to your dear Mother. May all her varied trials and endurances be speedily forgotten in the reception and enjoyment of the gospel of peace! But I know the difficulties—God Almighty Our Heavenly Father help you and her both.

Seeing that young Richardson needed companionship, Scott went on in this same letter to invite him to the Reserve, where he could mingle with the brethren. There was no doubt what the enthusiasm there would do for him.

On the Lord's-day 9th August I am to be in Warren where, I am sure, will be assembled a vast multitude of the Holy Brethren. I am personally acquainted with them all and should love above all things to have the pleasure of introducing you to every one of them. . . . If I don't see you against the 9th August, I shall perhaps come to see you and bring you to an Annual Meeting of the Brethren which is to take place on Friday the 28th August, when I bid you to be prepared to set out with me. I have many things to say to you. Write me immediately and I will answer it.[3]

In his loneliness, the young physician seized upon this proffered refuge with eagerness. The company of the faithful on the Reserve was precious and sustaining, but it was so far away! His medical duties would not allow him the time necessary for many of these long journeys.

The weeks wore on into months, and year's end approached without a reconciliation with his father. Formerly it had meant much to live only a few miles from his family home in Pittsburgh, but now his father's persistent hostility had turned this haven into a forbidden territory. This, together with his growing interest in and labor for the reformation, seemed to make a change in residence necessary.

When, toward the end of 1829, he learned that there was an opening for a physician in Wellsburg, Virginia, only seven miles from the Campbells at Bethany, it was without hesitation that he gave up his well-established practice in Carnegie and made ready to move to that city. It was no consideration for his future in the profession of medicine that led him to do this, for although he was a physician and would always remain one, he was now, first and foremost, a convinced and responsive servant of God, wholly devoted to the cause of a great reform.

"Think not that I am come to bring peace to the earth. I came not to bring peace, but a sword."

Chapter II

FIFTY-EIGHT FOURTH STREET

ROBERT was the first-born son of Nathaniel and Julia Logan Richardson. Nathaniel Richardson was a prosperous merchant. Calling himself "Ship's Chandeler," he presided over a store on Market Street, between Third and Fourth avenues. Here he sold rope, sails, rigging, and supplies for keelboats, flatboats, river steamers, and ocean-going vessels. He was a man of position and of good reputation, a charter member and vestryman of the Trinity Episcopal Church.[1] He had been in Pittsburgh since 1800 or earlier, having come directly from Ireland. In the New World he had prospered so that his name ranked with those of the other leading families in the city: Ammon, Bakewell, Bigham, Bruce, Cheverton, Childs, Craig, Dallas, Darlington, Hostetter, Kerr, McFarlane, Murray, Negley, Nevin, Passavant, Pears, Rea, Thaw, Wilkins, Van Bonnhorst.[2]

Julia Logan had come to the New World in 1800, accompanying her brother David, Jr., and her mother and father, also named Julia and David Logan. Her Irish parents had migrated from Londonderry. She had been married to Nathaniel Richardson in 1803.

Julia Logan Richardson possessed a refined temperament and a rich sympathy. Her cultivated taste found expression in music, art, and literature; she continued these Old World interests in her new home. The air of culture which surrounded her was not overstrained or posed, for it was her own native element; it provided the atmosphere in which gentle traits of character blossomed and where mutual consideration was a natural fruit.

Thus, in many ways, the personalities of Nathaniel and Julia Richardson were indeed complementary; for Nathaniel was a dignified businessman whose interests were largely materialistic. Beneath his normally polished exterior, there smoldered a hot Irish temper, which he managed to conceal from most of his friends, and most of the time from his family, and even from himself. He was as interested as Julia in fine things and fine living, but for different reasons. To him, these were of little value in themselves. They served, rather, as signs of his prosperity. They gave him distinction and made him a prominent citizen.

Robert, the first of twelve children, was born on September 26, 1806. All but one of his eleven brothers and sisters grew to maturity.

The mansion at 58 Fourth Street was the home of a genteel family in a rich neighborhood. Third, Fourth, and Fifth avenues, extending across lower Penn Street as far north as the Allegheny River, defined Pittsburgh's finest residential section. There were the mansions, the stables, and servant quarters of the wealthy. In this quiet, well-bred island of culture, businessmen isolated themselves and their families from the vulgarizing effects of their own commercial traffic and there preserved some of the charm and dignity of the Old World.

The Pittsburgh of Robert's boyhood was a gangling frontier town rapidly outgrowing its buckskins. By the time he was ten years of age the population of this "Gateway to the West" was about 8,000. The settlement presented a curious appearance, for the houses composing it were of all sorts: frame, brick, and stone, with a few log cabins built by the earliest settlers standing as reminders of their youth. These assorted domiciles possessed individuality; each stood on its lot without reference to its neighbors, cornerwise or endwise, just as its owner had pleased to build it.

There had been exciting things to see and do in this Pittsburgh in the early days of the century. At the point of the triangle of land on which the city stood, old Fort Pitt and crumbling Fort Duquesne moldered into ruin. With brothers and friends Robert had played French and English soldiers in these ruins, crawling into their empty powder magazines and old drains, or peering along a mock gun barrel around the broken walls, as imaginary Indians lurked just beyond musket fire.

At the river banks, on both the Monongahela and the Allegheny sides, it was possible to see long rows of keelboats and flatboats nudging the banks like gregarious water beetles. In the shipyards one could see the giant ribs of a future sailing vessel taking shape. Watching them rise, Robert had often seen visions of the Atlantic Ocean, to be reached by a long voyage down the Ohio and Mississippi and out through the Gulf of Mexico. It was always possible to see flatboats, or "Kentucky boats" as they were called, being banged together to accommodate the unending inland tide of people which poured across this wedge of land down the Ohio and on into the realm of the Indian and the buffalo.

At these same river docks, the lad had often watched graceful gondola-shaped keelboats put in on their return voyages from Cincinnati, carrying freight. He and his playmates had drawn back in respectful awe as the heroic, roistering keelboat men swaggered past. Perhaps the legendary Mike Fink was among them!

Robert had seen flatboats fitted out as floating department stores, and he had gazed admiringly at gleaming river steamers. These bright passenger boats, furnished with mahogany and rosewood furniture, and deeply carpeted, were America's inland luxury liners. While roads and railroads were still lacking in the wilderness, the rivers were broad, thronging arteries of traffic.

Familiar to him, too, was the music of hamebells on the harness of Conestoga horses. These magnificent six-horse teams, driven by burly German immigrants, pulled picturesque Conestoga wagons. Their boat-shaped, blue painted beds, red running gear, and flaring, white canvas covers made a colorful and exciting spectacle. He saw the daily stagecoaches dashing into town, only six days out of distant Philadelphia. Carrying the mails and twelve well-shaken passengers at $20 per fare, these queens of the road were a part of the restless movement of a migrating nation.

These sights, sounds, and adventures were all part of Robert's boyhood world, but they did not long occupy the center of attention. Gradually Julia Richardson's private world of culture won him over, and these outward excitements were pushed to the margins. With the complete acquiescence of his father, his mother had brought to this home private tutors in painting, music, and the French language. These interests came to displace the pure activism of boyhood, and Robert found that his mother's element was also natural to him. He learned to play the flute and the violin. So great was his aptness for music that he was even given his own Stradivarius. Sometimes he composed music for it, an enjoyment which persisted through the years. In the same way, painting also became a hobby. His early introduction to the French language made him as much at home in this tongue and literature as in his own; he read it with ease and with pleasure and spoke it fluently.

Robert also explored the world of books. In his father's large, spacious library he found himself contentedly at home. More and more of his leisure hours were spent here. Great minds from far countries and from the distant past invited him to the lure of learning. So habitual did his reading become, and so keen was his delight in it, that his father's severest punishments for childish misdemeanors took the form of exclusion from the library!

Likewise, Robert found fulfillment in his schoolwork. In 1815-17 he had been enrolled in an academy whose master was the wise and kindly Thomas Campbell. His father and a neighbor, James Irwin, had helped Mr. Campbell to gather the pupils the previous fall.[3] The Richardsons at that time knew or cared little about the mushrooming religious reformation which had sprung from Thomas Campbell's epochal *Declaration and Address,* published only six years before. Thomas Campbell was valued as a teacher of their children and as a guest and friend of the family.

Scarcely was Thomas Campbell settled when on December 14, 1815, his son, Alexander, had visited them in the Richardson household. This decisive and forceful young man, then twenty-seven, was also welcome as a friend. Neither Robert nor his family guessed his future fame, nor did they at this time even so much as glimpse the revolutionary character of his religious views. Although Robert could not fail to be impressed by the aristocratic face and bearing of the younger Campbell, he did not then see the way in which this man would come to occupy his future.

Alexander was on a three months' tour to raise a building fund for his church at Charlestown, Virginia (now Wellsburg, W. Va.). Nathaniel Richardson, as a supporter of churches and a patron of the decencies, made a generous gift of $20. This was the first contribution to the undertaking.[4]

Sitting under the tutelage of the elder Campbell and meeting the younger on the occasion of his brief visits, Robert formed a strong impression of the differing personalities of these two men.

> The father, full of affectionate sympathy and oversensitive in regard to the feelings of others, could not bear to inflict the slightest pain, and would rather withhold than confer a benefit which could be imparted only by wounding the recipient. The son, with more mastery of his emotional nature, could calmly contemplate the entire case, and, for the accomplishment of higher good, could resolutely inflict a temporary suffering. The former was cautious, forbearing, apologetic; the latter, decided, prompt and critical.

When Thomas Campbell left Pittsburgh in the summer of 1817, Robert was enrolled in a private academy conducted by George Forrester, who was also lay minister of a tiny independent congregation of "Haldane Christians," who met in the courthouse. At thirteen years of age, he was still a pupil in this same school when, in the summer of 1819, a young schoolmaster, recently arrived from Scotland, walked over the Allegheny Mountains and, as Forrester's assistant, straight into Robert's life. This teacher was Walter Scott, aged twenty-two.

Though separated by nine years and inhabiting the respective worlds of early youth and young manhood, these two found a mystical kinship of spirit. Robert yielded himself gladly to the rigorous discipline of the new schoolmaster.

"Mr. Scott possessed a peculiar tact as a teacher," he later reported, "having a quick perception of character, and knowing well how to excite the diligent, rouse the slothful and punish the disobedient. Though kind in his feelings, he pursued the strict system of discipline to which he had been accustomed in Europe, and which required *perfect* order and *accurate* recitations, or, as an alternative, the '*argumentum bacculinum*' [a caning, perhaps!]."[5]

To the French which he had learned earlier, Robert now added Greek and Latin. It was Scott's invariable practice to require "memorized recitations of portions of the ancient classic authors, as well as written translations of them." Robert, as one of the most gifted pupils, was also asked to commit nearly all the Greek New Testament to memory, until he could repeat, "chapter by chapter, the whole of the four gospels of Matthew, Mark, Luke, and John in the Greek language."[6]

Robert was now "friend and companion, as much as pupil," to Walter Scott. It was thus that he came to glimpse an aspect of his teacher's life that other pupils little suspected. Walter Scott was not only deeply religious; he was in the throes of an inner revolution of religious thinking. Revolting from sectarianism and orthodoxy, he was poring over his Bible far into the night, seeking a new insight into the meaning of Christianity. This quest finally drove him eastward, breaking up the school, and temporarily separating the friends. This was in the spring of 1821.

In the loss of his mentor and friend, Robert was desolate. Nathaniel Richardson moved quickly to remedy matters. Learning by mail that Scott's eastern quest had been fruitless, he enticed him back to Pittsburgh with the promise of an apartment in the Richardson home, a small school of fifteen of his most gifted pupils, and an inviting salary.[7]

When Scott returned, the pieces of his religious puzzle were beginning to fall into place. Though Robert did not then know all that was going on in his teacher's mind, he could see that its "ruling thought" was the personal creed of Christianity, "that Jesus is the Christ, the Son of God," which he called the "Golden Oracle," and which he believed to be the key to the Scriptures and the essence of the whole Christian religion.[8] The words "Jesus is the Christ" were written in chalk over the door of the schoolroom, on the inside. These bold white letters engraved themselves on Robert's mind, even before he could grasp their significance.

That winter Alexander Campbell came to visit, and a meeting took place between him and Walter Scott. Robert witnessed this meeting, which was the beginning of a lifelong friendship. Both these men were to become increasingly involved in his own affairs. Though Robert did not then realize it, both men were absorbed by the cause of church reform and found themselves in amazing agreement on such matters. It pleased him more than a little that these two friends of his had met and that they were drawn to one another. Outwardly, he noticed, they had little in common. Young Campbell was tall and athletic, possessed of strong animal spirits. Scott, on the contrary, was slight in build; he looked more like a recluse or a scholar. He detected in Campbell none of the lyrical, poetic temperament which he knew so well in Scott. Campbell seemed to him to have the most massively intellectual and coldly logical mind he had ever known. Scott, too, was logical and rational; but his was a flashing brilliance, like that of a waxing and waning bonfire, depending upon a strong draft from his emotions. Campbell's mind shone like the unblinking stare of the sun, depending only upon itself for its light. Strange that these two should be drawn together! Perhaps it was because they were complementary, and that in their very differences there was a harmonious blending. Anyway, Robert was glad they had become friends.

The young Richardson continued to spend many hours with his teacher, hours beyond the requirements of the schoolroom. Nathaniel Richardson had a small farm on the outskirts of the city, located in what is now the very heart of downtown Pittsburgh. In the evening, when the lessons were over, Robert would sometimes walk with the brooding Scott out to this farm. On one occasion, when Robert had plucked a rose and presented it to him, Scott, disclosing his religious preoccupation, took it with a question: "Do you know, my dear, why in the Scriptures Christ is called the Rose of Sharon?"

When Robert could make no immediate answer, Scott replied for him, "It is because the rose of Sharon has no thorns." Then he broke into a poetic discussion of the character of Christ and passed on to the power of the Creator which the beauty and perfection of the rose suggested.[9]

Although Robert had a connection with the Episcopal church and his father was a vestryman there, this formal religion meant little to him. It was Scott who quickened the spark of interest; at the same time, he never sought to make a proselyte of his pupil. Nevertheless, a seed had been planted by those gentle hands, and under the warming influence of that friendship, it would grow and eventually bear fruit.

Robert Richardson had reached his sixteenth year. Refined, artistic, gifted son of a gentle mother; accurate and precise scholar of an exacting teacher; considerate member of a large household; well-bred, well-born heir of a respected father; citizen of a bustling city on the threshold of a frontier; friend of men who were to become great; talented in measure suspected by others but as yet not fully discovered to himself, his future loomed before him, promising and alluring but undefined.

Chapter III

CHEMISTRY, MEDICINE, AND GOD

Events took a new turn for Robert in the winter of 1822-23. On January 30, 1823, Walter Scott was married to Sarah Whitsette[1] and moved from his apartment in the Richardson mansion to set up housekeeping. This change deprived the sixteen-year-old boy of a constant companionship upon which he had come to depend. Mr. Scott had now become "Walter" to him, and the separation was painful.

At the same time, the eldest son of Nathaniel Richardson was making his initial adjustment as a student in the newly formed Western University of Pennsylvania, (now the University of Pittsburgh). This school of college rank had received its charter from the Pennsylvania legislature on February 18, 1819, and, with its faculty installed, had begun its first session in the fall of 1822. Thus the old Pittsburgh Academy, chartered thirty-five years before, passed on up to university status. The faculty, with the eminent Dr. George Stevenson as president of the Board of Trustees, was composed of five professors: Rev. Robert Bruce, principal and professor of natural philosophy, chemistry, mathematics; Rev. John Black, professor of ancient language and classical literature; Rev. E. P. Swift, professor of moral science and the general evidences of Christianity; Rev. Joseph McElroy, professor of rhetoric and belles-lettres; and Rev. Charles B. Maguire, professor of modern languages and universal grammar. Robert's course included English, rhetoric, classical languages, and science, with a special concentration in chemistry.

The professor who influenced the young scholar most was Robert Bruce, principal and professor of science. He was a graduate of the University of Edinburgh, where he had studied under Dugald Stewart, of the Scottish "Common Sense School" of philosophy. He held the pastorate of the First Associated Church of Pittsburgh (Presbyterian) and was forty-four years of age. Men in all walks of life, said a contemporary, "pronounce him the most learned, the most sincere, the most kindly man they have ever met."

Scarcely less important to Robert was Professor Black. He was born in county Antrim, Ireland. After graduating from the University of Glasglow, he had come on to America to teach in the University of Philadelphia, and thence to the ministry of the Reformed Presbyterian Church of Pittsburgh. This classical scholar was a writer, as well, contributing freely to local magazines. As a teacher, he was a constant stimulus and delight to his students. Possessing little patience with dull scholars, he had at the same time an irrepressible sense of humor. His students watched eagerly for "the significant twinkle of his eye, the corrugation of his brow, which betrayed his internal glee."[2]

In these fields of learning, especially in the exact disciplines of science, Robert Richardson found himself happily at home. Under these favorable conditions, a love for precision quickly disclosed itself. His notebooks were accurate and neat. A Greek sample, dealing with the opening section of Matthew's Gospel, looks flawless enough to have come from a printing press. Not only is the script clear and faultless, but the statement of usage and construction is such as to attract the attention of careful scholars. The same is true of a notebook kept while perusing a course in Scottish history.

Always an obedient and respectful son, Robert was never more so than toward the religious wishes of his parents. With them he attended church regularly at "The Old Round Church" of the Episcopalians, where his father was a charter member and vestryman. Walter Scott's influence had made him much more attentive to religious matters. The result was that he began reading the Scriptures and paying more attention to his prayers and to sermons.

The Episcopal church had erected a queer, octagonal building in 1805, the year of its organization, and Pittsburghers immediately dubbed it "The Old Round Church." It stood on a triangular lot now defined by Liberty Street, Sixth Avenue, and Wood Street. Rev. John Taylor, eminent rector of this congregation, also published an almanac, forecasting the weather one year in advance. He became something of an awe-inspiring oracle to the whole city when he once prophesied a snowstorm in mid-June, and hit it exactly![3]

The Episcopalians continued to worship in "The Old Round Church" until 1825. Up until 1830, in all Pittsburgh there were only ten church buildings, although there were fifteen congregations, some of which met in the courthouse and in private homes.

Meantime the vigorous John Henry Hopkins became rector. He had left the iron furnace to study law, and had then given up the bar to enter the ministry. When he moved from Pittsburgh in 1831, it was to accept a call to the Trinity Church of Boston. He was later to become bishop of Vermont. Before he left Pittsburgh, however, he led his people in building a new Trinity Church on a Pennsylvania land grant, allotted for the purpose.[4]

Robert's deepened religious interest encouraged his mother and other relatives to hope that he would enter the ministry, but in this hope they had not watched their candidate closely enough. The young man was attracted to Christianity but strangely disquieted by its Episcopalian form.

There was another reason why the urgings of his friends in the church were unavailing. He was embarrassed and retiring by nature, and the prospect of leading a life so public, so constantly before great throngs of people, together with the necessity of continual speaking, dismayed and terrified him.

So it came about that he not only did not decide for the ministry, but that he even delayed his confirmation from season to season. Finally, he had put it off until he was eighteen years of age. The combined pressure of father and rector was then brought to bear upon him, with the result that he yielded in 1824, and at Easter of that year was confirmed by Rev. William White, bishop of Pennsylvania, with Rev. John Henry Hopkins assisting.

At the same time that his enthusiasm remained unquickened in the church, it was vibrantly responsive in the classrooms of the Western University of Pennsylvania. Chemistry, in particular, fascinated him. As the time for the completion of his course approached, a decision concerning his lifework became imperative. His interest in chemistry pointing the way, he chose medicine.

Leaving the university in 1824 or 1825, he began the specific preparation then in vogue to fit him for his profession. In his case, this meant "reading medicine" under the personal oversight of a successful physician. The Richardson family chose Dr. Peter Mowry, himself a former pupil of Dr. Nathaniel Bedford, who had been Pittsburgh's first physician. It is also significant that Dr. Mowry was a vestryman of the Trinity Episcopal Church and a trustee of Western University.

Dr. Mowry was at the head of his profession. In a day before antiseptics and anesthetics, when much witchcraft was practiced in the name of science by other members of the calling, he was wise and clear-sighted.

He always sought to impress upon his students the great responsibility of the profession they had chosen. He advised hospital experience as the best way to become a skilled physician. On one occasion he said: "God help the quack, who with little knowledge and much impudence rushes in where conscientious men fear to enter."[5]

"Reading medicine" was strenuous activity. Besides the constant poring over technical books and journals, it involved practical assistance to the physician, some of it of a rather menial sort. It was no little chore for Robert, reared in a wealthy home, with the continual care of servants, to "clean the office, brush the boots and clothing of the doctor and take care of the horse and stable." He became a sort of junior physician and handyman, learning by doing. It was not long until Dr. Mowry was relying on him to pull the teeth of dental patients and to do much of the bleeding. Bleeding was based upon the current theory that it drained impurities from the body. The treatment of nearly all ailments included bleeding. Even a common head cold might call for bleeding a patient from seven to twenty times within a few days.

Bleeding was done both with a knife and by the use of leeches. In the spring of the year people were thought to have too much blood or blood that was too thick. This condition was remedied by bleeding. Sometimes an individual was annoyed with attacks of dizziness; again bleeding was prescribed. The attending physician carried a small china bowl which held between a cup and a pint. The amount of blood taken from the patient, determined by the size of his body and the malignancy of the attack, varied from one to two bowls. During the process of the operation the patient bared his arm, allowing the incision to be made in forearm or upper arm; then he took a firm grip on a broom handle to hurry the flow and make it steady. The junior physician did all of this, at first, under careful supervision. Later, it was necessary for Dr. Mowry to do no more than indicate the amount of blood to be let.

Robert was also taught to "cup," a treatment consisting of raising a blister under a heated tea cup placed on the forehead, to cure headaches and some fevers. The collecting, drying, and grinding of herbs and roots also fell to him. All medicines, even those which were purchased rather than brought from the fields, were obtained in crude form, so that they had to be ground with mortar and pestle and prepared in the doctor's office. Field trips included the finding and collecting of leeches in the neighboring streams.

In addition to these duties, the neophyte physician chopped wood, ran errands, accompanied the doctor, carrying his lantern by night and his saddlebags by day.

His rigorous training acquainted young Richardson with all phases of a physician's work. Among the customs of the day, none was more satirical than that which required the attending physician of a patient who had died to lead the funeral procession on the way to the grave!

This apprenticeship was a strenuous, exacting life, and Dr. Mowry was at no pains to make it easy for his student. By midwinter of 1825-26, Robert's health was broken. Mostly the trouble had to do with his eyes. As a result of inadequate pigmentation, his eyes were oversensitive to light. Constant reading irritated these organs. Often he had to leave his studies to bathe his eyes in cold water in order to gain temporary relief, and occasionally the pain reached such a pitch that he was forced to give up reading and writing altogether for long periods of days and weeks. He had now reached such a time, the first of many enforced vacations from his beloved books. Medical science of the day diagnosed the ailment as "amaurosis." The weakness of Robert's eyes led him to form the habit of half-closing the lids to shut out the glare of light. The only time he opened them wide was during periods of mirth, and then it could be seen that they were a beautiful hazel in color. These weary, suffering orbs refused to do any more.

Robert's father and mother were agreed that he needed a period of rest. He was sent, accordingly, to "Ravens Vale," the farm of the Blairs', who were warm family friends of theirs, living near Elizabeth, Pennsylvania. There he was kept strictly away from books and lived much out of doors. Staying on from winter into spring, summer, and autumn, he lived around the whole farmer's clock of seasons and there acquired an undying love for the country and farming. He went sledding and hiking over the snow, or skating with the young people, and sat by the fire on winter evenings, exchanging stories with a merry company. Springtime came, and now he followed the plowman, and in the summer the reaper's swinging scythe. He took the cows to the pasture, or sauntered over the meadows and along the brooks. Sometimes an evening would be spent with jovial young people in dancing at home or at a neighbor's.

All of this was good medicine for the sick young doctor, and it was marvelously effective. By the fall of 1826 he was well and happy, and it was decided that it would be safe for him to return to his studies. He was only twenty then and he had already studied much beyond his years. Having glimpsed for a few months a world of youth and of activity that he had almost missed completely, he found himself reluctant to depart. With a wrench of the heart he contemplated the painful leave-takings and decided that he would not be able to go through with it; so, in lieu of a formal good-by, in the early morning hours of his last day, he left a poem on the dresser in his room and stole out of the house before the family was awake.

The Blair family, finding the poem, read it between smiles and tears. Afterward they had it printed in booklet form, both to prolong their own enjoyment of it and also to share it with their friends. "Lines written upon leaving Ravens Vale in the fall of 1826" began as follows:

> Sweet vale of peace! in lengthening shades,
> How fast thy beauteous landscape fades;
> And softly murmuring through the trees;
> How springs the gentle evening breeze;
> While lingering oft I turn to gaze
> On thee, loved scene of happy days,
> And mournfully with tearful eye,
> Long, a sad farewell to sigh.

The last of the 124 lines trailed away in melancholy moonlight:

> With evening dews each leaf is wet,
> In heaven each starry lamp is set,
> And in the east the rising moon
> Resumes her placid course, and soon
> Will silver all thy scenery
> And light me far away from thee!
>
> Sweet vale of peace! Though time no more
> Me to thy happy fields restore
> Yet though afar from thee removed
> I'll cherish still thy memory loved.

In conformity with the customary pattern of training, Robert was now ready to take a course of lectures in medical school. Few doctors bothered to go through the formality of acquiring an M.D. degree. So Robert Richardson was duly matriculated in the School of Medicine of the University of Pennsylvania at Philadelphia. He attended for the school year of 1826-27.[6]

In the spring of 1827 he returned to Pittsburgh to set up a copractice for a few months with an established physician, whose name is unfortunately lost from the record. Gradually he accustomed himself to respond when called "Doctor" and at length got himself into the swing of his practice.

Before long, feeling sufficiently prepared to strike out independently, he moved to Carnegie, a village thirteen miles from Pittsburgh, and set up practice in what proved to be a predominantly Presbyterian community. There being no Episcopal church there, he united with the Presbyterians, without relinquishing his Episcopalian connection with the family church at home.

Although he was now only twenty-one years old, Dr. Robert Richardson quickly became popular, and his practice grew. Emphasizing preventive hygiene and sanitation and practicing little surgery, he kept to conservative and common-sense lines, with good results. His earnings, gathered in fees of fifteen and twenty-five cents, were netting him a modest living. He was established.

It was in the midst of this busy practice that Walter Scott re-entered his life. His friend had left Pittsburgh in the spring of 1826 to set up a church and a school in Steubenville, Ohio. Thence he had gone the following year to become evangelist of the Mahoning Baptist Association in the Western Reserve.

When Scott rode out to visit him in the spring of 1829, Robert at once detected a suppressed excitement in his old friend and quickly felt that he was greeting a prophet. The last pieces of Scott's religious puzzle had fallen into place nearly two years before, and he had been preaching a "Restored Gospel" to aroused audiences all over northeastern Ohio. The Baptist churches of that region were electric with expectancy, seething with study and discussion, and he had baptized two thousand converts.

Scott explained to his friend that this was no repetition of old-style revivals. It was something new in modern Christianity, straight out of the pages of the New Testament. The Campbells had been laboring for twenty years with much success in restoring the "Ancient Order" in the church—weekly Communion, baptism by immersion, a plurality of elders, local church government, the priesthood of all believers, discarding creeds and theological tests of "faith." It had remained for him, Scott said, to restore the "Ancient Gospel," by which men gained entrance into this "Ancient Order"! It all went back to his discovery of the "Golden Oracle." Accepting Jesus as Lord was the key to Christianity. How was this done? The Book of Acts offers the clue! Men are asked by the apostles to do three things: to *believe*, on the basis of the facts of the New Testament; to *repent*; and to be *baptized*. God, in turn, promises to do three things: to *remit sins*; to grant the gift of the *Holy Spirit*; and to impart *life eternal*.

When Scott had gone, Robert could not get the visit and the excitement out of his mind. In his spare hours over the next few days he studied his Greek Bible minutely. Come to think of it, he had learned to read Greek at Walter's hands. He went over the ground of their recent discussions, checking at every point. The result was plain.

He became fully convinced that in both the Septuagint Old Testament and the Greek New Testament the words *bapto* and *baptidzo* meant to immerse, or dip; and that "to translate them thus would make complete sense and harmony of the passage in which they occur; whereas, to introduce the idea of sprinkling, would frequently make absolute nonsense of scripture." He also found that "faith and repentance were absolute prerequisites for christian baptism" and that the word of God commanded baptism as prerequisite to the remission of sins and the gift of the Holy Spirit.[7]

No sooner was he convinced by his studies that Scott was right than he decided to act. Saddling his horse, he rode straight toward the Western Reserve, and directly to Scott's home at Canfield. Walter was not at home, but he found him on the third day, and at the end of 120 miles, with his colaborer William Hayden in Shalersville. He arrived on Sunday, at two o'clock in the afternoon, just after the audience had been dismissed and when the two evangelists were preparing to immerse six converts in the near-by Cuyahoga River.

Pressing through the crowd, Robert first surprised Scott with his presence and then overwhelmed him with his request to be baptized. He had never witnessed an immersion until he saw those which preceded his own and he had never heard a preacher of "the Reformation" until he listened to William Hayden's address at the conclusion of the ceremony.[8]

Now, for the first time in his life, religion, which had both fascinated and eluded him, came intimately near. Before this new interest, even chemistry and medicine faded. His newly found happiness could not serve as a simple embellishment of his old manner of living. It demanded a change, a complete revolution.

Back in Carnegie, he devoted much time to getting his bearings within his new cause. He now learned that a "Reformation of the Nineteenth Century" had been afoot for more than twenty years. In 1809 Thomas Campbell, his own teacher, had written a manifesto of Christian union, called the *Declaration and Address*, which he now read with mounting surprise and admiration. Casting off creeds as tests of fellowship, distinguishing between essentials and nonessentials, and calling for a return to biblical simplicity and to charity in all things, this document was the charter of a unified Christendom! Similarly, a movement of reform had arisen in Kentucky in 1804, following the great Cane Ridge meeting. A group of Presbyterian ministers including Barton Warren Stone had written "The Last Will and Testament of the Springfield Presbytery," in which they, too, called for church reform, along much the same lines. Alexander Campbell had become the champion and leader of the Virginia and Pennsylvania movement; his adherents were known to his bitterest enemies as "Campbellites" and to his friends as "Reformers." About this time they were beginning to call themselves "Disciples of Christ." Stone's movement used the simple name "Christians."

Both movements were publishing magazines for the propagation of their cause. Stone's *Christian Messenger* had exerted a strong influence in Kentucky for two years, and Alexander Campbell's militant *Christian Baptist* was read by an amazingly large audience in the eastern half of the nation and had spread his name and views throughout that part of America since 1823.

At the same time, Alexander Campbell's fame as a debater was mounting—and this was happening in an era much given to the exercise of oratory and the drama of public debate. In March, 1820, he had debated with Rev. John Walker at Mount Pleasant, Ohio, on the subjects and action of baptism. In October, 1823, he had debated with Rev. W. I. Maccalla at Washington, Kentucky, on the purpose or design of baptism. More recently, this very spring, on April 13-22, 1829, Alexander Campbell had achieved a *tour de force* in his masterly defeat of the famous social reformer and atheist, Robert Owen, in their debate on "The Evidences of Christianity."

Having met these reformers in the quiet parlor of the Richardson home, Robert had not guessed the extent of their influence or the radical character of their interests. Now, he discovered that his friend Walter Scott had become intimately associated with both wings of this reformatory impulse. On the Western Reserve he had welded "Christians" and "Reformers" into a team to "restore the Ancient Gospel" and was sweeping thousands of new adherents into the swelling tide of nonsectarian Christianity.[9] With his fiery zeal and his matchless oratory, Scott was the evangelistic partner of what was soon to become known as the "big four": the Campbells, father and son, Barton W. Stone, and Walter Scott.

Here, Robert felt, was a cause which was not only righteous, but also one destined to take everything before it. Already it numbered between 12,000 and 20,000 adherents.[10] America was a land of new beginnings; it was not too much to hope that its frontiers would also become the place where divided Protestantism would be transformed into a united Christendom!

So great was his zeal for what he learned, and so deep was his inward happiness at his own conversion, that the young doctor overcame his terror before audiences and went out as an ambassador of the cause. Soon he had gathered and organized a church![11] From this church at Carnegie, lines of influence reached out through relatives to Washington County, near the place where the *Declaration and Address* had been written. There, with the aid of some of Thomas Campbell's staunch friends, James and John McElroy, he established and ministered to a second church.

The physician was not a gifted public speaker. He was timid and hesitant before an audience. While getting into the opening part of an address or sermon, he cleared his throat a great deal and stopped and started like a lurching stagecoach drawn by a frightened team. Discerning hearers quickly saw that he was an artist in the choice of words; but many in his audiences could never penetrate beyond the nervous cough and the monotonous, undramatic delivery to the fire and beauty which glowed beneath. He did not speak because he liked it but because he was now taken captive by a momentous purpose and could not keep silent.

The doctor was a busy man. Keeping up with his medical practice and practicing his religion as an active agent of church reform occupied his nights and his days, his weekdays and his Lord's days; but he was well content. In fact, he was happier than he had ever been.

He was so busy that he did not have time to go home to tell his family the news, so he wrote a letter and dispatched it by the post. His action had been so precipitate, and the reasons for it so patently convincing to him, that he had not even thought to consult their wishes before he undertook the trip to Shalersville. And it did not once occur to him that his father might be offended.

CHAPTER IV

REBEKAH

DOCTOR RICHARDSON came to Wellsburg in January
of 1830. This valley town, located about forty miles
down the Ohio from its source and just north of the
mouth of Buffalo Creek, was shouldered up against the
river by giant overlooking hills which allowed only a
narrow strip of level land for the settlement. That settlement had been laid out in 1790 by Charles Prather on
481 acres of land. In honor of its founder the Virginia
legislature named it Charlestown, but later withdrew the
name because it was so easily confused with Charleston,
and renamed it Wellsburg in honor of Prather's son-in-
law, Alexander Wells.

Wellsburg, at the time when Richardson moved there,
boasted a Methodist Episcopal church, built in 1816, and
the Baptist church which Alexander Campbell and John
Brown had erected in the same year with contributions to
which Nathaniel Richardson had made the first gift!
There was a glass factory and a market house. John
Brown, who was Alexander Campbell's father-in-law,
owned a carding mill and grist mill, run by horse power.
Wellsburg had its own boat yards. At the mouth of the
Buffalo Creek, schooners were built which later sailed the
open seas as far as Liverpool, England, laden with flour
ground in Wellsburg mills. The town also had a busy
river dock catering to the flourishing trade of flatboats
and keelboats.

A four-page, four-column weekly newspaper, the Wellsburg *Gazette*, kept everyone informed of the news. This paper advertised hotel rooms at the Granite House and the Virginia House, boosted the stock of the Wellsburg and Washington (Pa.) Turnpike Company, and informed its readers that a riverbank wall was about to be erected along the town with money raised by a state lottery.

Robert Richardson associated himself at once with the Baptist church of the "Reformers." Both Thomas and Alexander Campbell worshiped here, and the doctor found himself included in the warmest possible fellowship. He was soon an intimate part of the congregation.

The same ties took him often to Bethany and into the company of those who found their way to Mr. Campbell's hospitality. Here he had the privilege of talking with Thomas Campbell and many of the influential leaders in the current reformation. It was here also that he was fortunate enough, on rare occasions, to meet with Walter Scott and renew the bonds of their earlier friendship. Discussions within this charmed social circle were lively and stimulating to the new advocate of reform.[1]

Robert Richardson was now in his twenty-fourth year. He was five feet ten inches in height and weighed about 130 pounds.[2] He walked rigidly erect, with his shoulders square, and his head high. This, together with his slender build, gave him the appearance of great height. Contemporary witnesses tell us that he was a little taller than Alexander Campbell. His voice was thin and naturally pitched in a high key. He spoke in a conversational tone, which sometimes deepened into an expression of intense emotion.[3] His manner was reserved and courteous; he gave the impression of possessing immense inner reservoirs of knowledge and of personal power.

Caring little about stylish dress, he garbed himself modestly, frequently wearing a Prince Albert, which the times dictated for a physician or other professional man. Although he was always neat, he could never understand why anyone should preen himself to attract attention to his clothes. During the winter months his habitual headgear was a beaver or a felt hat, while the summer found him wearing a Panama. He was never known to don a cap, for he felt that this article of clothing was horribly ugly. Like other gentlemen, he wore fine boots, which he removed with a bootjack.

Like most physicians, whose calls took them over a wide domain, Dr. Richardson rode horseback nearly everywhere he went. He hated riding in a carriage or buggy; riding in them made him "seasick"; but on his horse he was comfortable and happy. The tall, slender, quiet man riding astride his faithful mount soon became a familiar figure in Wellsburg and its vicinity. In his saddlebags he carried the usual remedies, a very few instruments, the bleeding bowl, and his daybook.

This daybook reveals that his first visit in Wellsburg was made on February 13, 1830. Almost from the first he enjoyed a good practice. Office calls and home visits kept increasing in number. Some patients paid, others were billed, and still others gave notes. Some accounts the doctor marked "lost," while other accounts he canceled out with the expressive word, "forgiven." His charges were uniformly moderate. With great care he tabulated each visit, the nature of the ailment, and the remedy prescribed—usually in Latin.

Having been schooled by the wise Peter Mowry, Dr. Richardson's practice of medicine differed widely from that of most physicians. He followed common-sense lines rather than the pedantic dogma of "the schools." With a patient and his family he conversed freely but in a slow manner. He never grew excited. Believing much of the medical practice of his day to be unscientific sham, he was plain and straightforward in his diagnosis and prescriptions. He spent much time teaching his patient the causes and conditions of illness; ignorance he conceived to be a great enemy to good health. Water supply, sewage and garbage disposal, bedroom ventilation, careful eating, regular habits, ample exercise, and a clean heart—these were the topics which he frequently discussed with patients as essentials of good health and the enjoyment of life. In his teaching he stressed right thinking, for he realized the close relation between mind and body, and he believed that "a merry heart doeth good like a medicine." Into the well-kept ledger he frequently entered after a patient's name only three words: "Visit and advice."

He decried "specifics" in medicine, refusing to countenance "sure cures" for baffling ailments. Instead, he trusted much to nature to restore its own balances. This being so, it is not surprising that he used home remedies in a large way. Teas such as were usually concocted by housewives received his sanction. Calomel, generally a highly touted remedy, he refused to use. He relied much upon herbs which he himself gathered from the fields or which the relatives of his patients were told to gather under his direction. For colds in the chest or for sprained ligaments and muscles, he advocated plasters and poultices. Headaches he treated by placing the pounded leaves of horseradish on the sufferer's forehead or the back of his neck. Turpentine and lard was a common concoction which he used on the chest and throat of those victimized by severe colds. This application he bound into place with a large piece of red flannel.

Wherever he went in his busy practice, he kept an exact record of each case, never relying on his memory. In his daily ledger he set down the ailment diagnosed under the date when he saw the patient, the medicines which he prescribed, and the exact amount of the dosage.

Never posing as a surgeon, although he did the minor and emergency surgery which seemed necessary, he removed surface growths such as warts, moles, wens, and surface tumors, and lanced abscesses, boils, and carbuncles. He reduced fractures and set dislocated joints. But he was ever cautious, taking no chances with new procedures which had not been adequately tested and tried.

In keeping with the practice of all physicians in his day, Dr. Richardson often turned dentist. "Ext. Dentis, 25 cents" was entered frequently in his daily ledger. Many who had nursed aching teeth for days finally mustered the needed courage and came to get relief. The doctor's tooth pulling was far from painless! Knowing nothing of treating the gums or using a needle to deaden pain, he simply made the extraction with an old-fashioned forceps, which he operated with a sort of cantilever twist, bringing out both the tooth and a yelp of pain from the patient simultaneously. The idea of saving teeth was not given a place in the health economy of that day. Physicians were expected to practice destructive dentistry, and Dr. Richardson did his share.

His medical ledger, which he kept with extreme care, shows some of his fees: pulling a tooth ("extracti dentis") was 25 cents; visit (regular) 50 cents to $3.00, depending on the distance and the time consumed; visits at night ("Noctu") were more expensive; vaccination ranged from 75 cents to $1.00; "excisio Tumor" he posted at $2.00. He even engaged to attend the family of Joe Perry, Wellsburg, one entire year for a covering fee of $10— an early application of the principle of health insurance! He sold medicines and drugs to his patients at current prices, ranging from 18 cents to 62½ cents and 93 cents per portion, depending on the remedy.

If it was from practicing medicine that Robert made his living, it was in the current religious reformation that he found his life. Almost at once he began writing for Disciple magazines. Alexander Campbell abandoned the seven-year-old *Christian Baptist* in this year and began publishing the *Millennial Harbinger*. The first monthly issue appeared on Monday, January 4, 1830. The prospectus declared:

> This work shall be devoted to the destruction of sectarianism, infidelity, and antichristian doctrine and practice. It shall have for its object the developement and introduction of that political and religious order of society called THE MILLENNIUM, which will be the consummation of that ultimate amelioration of society proposed in the Christian Scriptures.[4]

Richardson had written some articles for the *Christian Baptist* and he was pleased that he could now continue his contributions in a magazine of more ample dimensions. The *Harbinger* was to be issued in monthly editions of forty-eight large duodecimo pages; at $2.00 per year if paid in advance, or $2.50 if payment was deferred until the end of the year.

In the May number of the *Millennial Harbinger,* there appeared the first of eight articles on the general subject of "Regeneration," written by Robert Richardson. These he signed with his pen name, "Discipulus." This series of articles, seen and read by Alexander Campbell in advance of publication, broke mental ground for the Bethany editor.[5] Richardson had taken a unique view of regeneration, one such as only a physician would have seen. Having officiated at the birth of numerous babies, his mind responded to the phrase "spiritual birth" in terms of physical birth. Although the birth of a baby was a cataclysmic experience, it did not change the *nature* of the infant, he pointed out; it merely changed his *relations* or his *state*. He was the same infant in or out of the womb, but he was not in the same *state,* for his *relations* were different. The actual beginning of the baby started long before its birth. In the same way, "in the spiritual world, a man who is born again has come forth from water as from the womb, having been previously begotten by the Spirit."[6] This idea was luminous and inviting to Mr. Campbell and it set his mind to working along a new line, with the result that he began writing an extra for the *Millennial Harbinger,* his now famous *Extra on the Remission of Sins,* producing it within two weeks. This sixty-page document had a remarkable circulation and a wide influence. Mr. Campbell later incorporated it into his book of theology, *The Christian System.*

Characteristically, Robert Richardson had seen more intimately into a rather minute aspect of a subject, and his scientific mind had yielded a new insight. Alexander Campbell, just as characteristically, had immediately envisioned that new insight in its larger implications. Having seen a whole new domain of truth illuminated by the doctor's pen, he had then taken up his own pen to write upon the subject with the bold sweep and the panoramic breadth which distinguished the literary presentation of his religious views. It was beginning already to be apparent that writer Richardson and editor Campbell would make a good team.

Now, articles began fairly to tumble from the young doctor's pen. Over the nom de plume of "Alumnus" he wrote "Order Is Heaven's First Law" for the March *Harbinger* of 1831. Still over that name, there followed a new series on "Counterfeits," exposing fraudulent forms of Christianity.

His friend Walter Scott, the cyclonic evangelist, was now living in Cincinnati and was there publishing his own monthly magazine, called the *Evangelist* (begun Jan., 1832). For this organ of the "Ancient Gospel," Robert began to write in its very first year.

The first volume of the *Evangelist* carried three articles from "Discipulus." In these articles he dealt with miscellaneous topics. New ideas, he said in the first of these articles, always encounter opposition, noting that the new ideas of the current reformation were being accorded the same sort of reception. Nevertheless, opposition was far from being the full story: "The whole of our country is ripe for the harvest, and we have nothing to do but to thrust in our sickles and an abundant crop will be

gathered."[7]   In fact, to find a parallel to the stirrings of
this day, one would have to go back to the New Testament itself.

In his second article for the *Evangelist*, "Discipulus"
touched upon one of the Disciples' weak spots, Christian
stewardship:

> A few choice spirits among us . . . are preaching and teach-
> ing by day and night, spending their time . . . to build up and
> set in order the church of God; and who among us *love them
> but in word?*—who love them in *deed*, and in *truth?* . . .
>
> Brethren, the fountain of christian benevolence is dried up
> among us. . . . The great christian virtue of contributing to the
> necessities of those who are bearing reproach and shame, on ac-
> count of Christ, and who are devoting their lives to the work of
> converting the world to primitive christianity, is lost sight of.[8]

In the same series he also commented on "walking by
faith," declaring that "faith is one thing," while "walking
by faith another." "Too many walk by *sight or by feeling*, and not by *faith*."[9]

The doctor's meticulous attention to detail is noticed in
his own copy of Walter Scott's *Evangelist* for January,
1833.   In that issue an unsigned article on the topic
"Jesus" appeared.   With his proofreader's pencil, the
doctor deleted the title and supplied another, "All-
sufficiency of Christ"; he then corrected several typographical errors and finally wrote underneath the initials
"R. R."   In fact, he made his own marginal corrections
throughout on all the pages of this issue, and at the
bottom of the last page wrote this notation, "73 errors
in this number!"

Walter Scott, the preacher and evangelist, did not have the patient exactitude required of a good proofreader; misspellings and inaccuracies crept past him, but the young physician had just the traits that the Cincinnati editor lacked. We are not surprised, therefore, when we learn that Walter Scott had visited Robert in Wellsburg the year before he launched the *Evangelist* and had expressly urged him to move to Carthage, adjacent to Cincinnati, where he could set up a practice of medicine and serve as coeditor of the new magazine. Richardson did not at once respond to his old friend's invitation, but he did continue to write, both for the *Millennial Harbinger* and for the *Evangelist*. In the latter publication, three articles on "Conscience" appeared. A January letter addressed to "Dear Walter" informed him, "I am writing a little piece for you which I hope to send shortly."

Walter Scott was himself the chief reason why his friend Robert had not moved to Carthage immediately. Early in 1830 the Mahoning evangelist had been in Wheeling, where he had met the Encell family. A few days later he stopped in Wellsburg to visit the young physician.

"I have just met the prettiest girl I have ever seen!" he announced.

Sensing that there was more behind the words than appeared on the surface, Robert gave him instant attention. "Where?" he asked.

"In Wheeling," Scott replied.

"Who was she? What was her name?" Robert asked.

"Rebekah Encell," his friend answered.

Robert knew the name of Encell. John Encell, Rebekah's father, had built one of Wellsburg's first glass houses. Together with John Brown and Alexander Campbell, he had been one of the officers of the Wellsburg church. And then, suddenly, he had died in 1829, and shortly afterward his family had moved to Wheeling.

It was not long until Robert Richardson had occasion to visit the brethren in Wheeling. He contrived an introduction to Rebekah. She was all that Walter had said she would be and more. Robert fell instantly in love with her.

Rebekah was tall, slender, and supple in build, graceful and unaffected as well as amazingly beautiful. Her disposition was gay and lively. She was joyously at home and happy in the company of other young people. She was just ten years younger than Robert, having also been born in Pittsburgh, September 10, 1816. In terms of the day, though only fourteen, she was of marriageable age.

There followed an intensive courtship, lasting about a year. It was April 10, 1831, when Alexander Campbell himself united Rebekah and Robert in holy wedlock. The doctor's ledger reveals entries for April 8 and 11, but none for April 9 and 10. It seems that he was occupied by other matters during these two days "out of the office"!

Robert brought his bride to live in Wellsburg. This was her old home. Having left the city quite recently, she was known and loved there. Since Rebekah was also a member of the reformation, they immediately took a prominent place in the work of the Wellsburg church.

Shortly after the marriage, Robert's mother and his sister Jane came down to Wellsburg to visit them. His father was still estranged. Jane, a truly dignified Richardson, was a member of the choir of the Trinity Episcopal Church. During the family worship which occurred in the midst of this visit, a small mouse came out and played around Jane's chair. Rebekah, seeing it, was convulsed with glee; unable to contain herself, she burst out into uncontrolled laughter, interrupting the devotions. This conduct somewhat shocked the sedate guests. They went away, not too sure that Robert had chosen the right bride.

But concerning Rebekah Encell Richardson, the church at Wellsburg had no doubts. She had been known to them since childhood. She and Robert were taken into the bosom of the church and were soon busy in its activities. On September 6, 1832, the brethren passed this resolution: "That a congregational record be henceforth duly kept in a book provided for the purpose, and that R. Richardson be requested to act as clerk." Finding the church without any previous records, he procured a minute book and wrote in it a sketch of the previous history of the congregation, bringing it up to date and continuing the record carefully from the date of his appointment until he left the community. The same meeting that appointed him clerk also named him a member of a committee on "godly edification." Other members were Thomas Campbell, John Brown, F. W. Emmons, and H. N. Bakewell. This committee was asked "to consult together and make such arrangements for the proper ordering of the public exercises of the church, the times of meeting, etc., as may tend to promote the edification of the disciples, by calling forth the gifts of each member for the benefit of all." This meeting also voted to ask "Father Campbell" to take up his residence in Wellsburg for the purpose of "assisting us in acquiring a knowledge of the scriptures and getting things into better order among us." To this request, Thomas Campbell acceded. On May 19, 1833, Robert Richardson's committee was reappointed and charged with the additional responsibility of disciplining offenders against the regulations of the church.

On April 12, 1834, a general meeting of messengers from thirteen congregations, called by the brethren in Wheeling, was held in Wellsburg. The purpose of this meeting was to develop a system of cooperation. This was the first group attempt among Disciples to create some plan of interchurch organization to promote united effort which would at the same time completely safeguard the autonomy of the local churches against any attempted domination by the central body. Robert Richardson attended this meeting as a delegate of the Wellsburg church.

While these events were taking place, there were happenings more private to the Richardson household, but not less important. Nathaniel Richardson II was born on January 13, 1833, son of the proud doctor who had delivered many babies, but never one so precious as this one! When Nathaniel I learned of this, his stubborn temper was unequal to the strain of natural affection, and the happiness of the fond parents was made to brim over in the reconciliation with little Nathaniel's grandfather. "A little child shall lead them."

It now became possible for them to make plans to accept Walter Scott's invitation to move to Carthage and assist him as coeditor of the *Evangelist*. Accordingly, on June 8, 1834, the Wellsburg church records report,

"Rob't. Richardson and Rebekah Richardson requested a letter to the church at Carthage, Ohio: which was granted." Thereupon Robert Richardson resigned as clerk, as a member of the committee on godly edification, and as a member of the Committee of Cooperating Churches. He was replaced by Archibald W. Campbell.[10]

Walter Scott, having in 1832 founded a flourishing church at Carthage, "seven miles along the Canal" from Cincinnati, had moved his family and his printing office to that village and now issued the *Evangelist* from that address. Yielding to the Carthage editor's urgent pressure, Dr. Richardson had decided to move to this village, become a medical partner to Dr. Wright, who was already established there, and to take up an editorial pen. Taking with him Rebekah and their first-born son and hugging to himself the joy of being again in the good graces of his father, he set out for this promised land with a singing heart.

CHAPTER V

MAN OF LETTERS

WHEN Robert, Rebekah, and little Nathaniel Richardson moved to Carthage early in June, 1834, it was to a respectable Christian community, located only seven miles from Cincinnati, directly on the Miami Canal. Two years before, in a matter of months, Walter Scott's phenomenal evangelistic powers had transformed a roistering, profane frontier town into a sober and civilized community. Cincinnati itself was a city larger than Pittsburgh, unashamedly calling herself "Queen City of the West." In the nation the hour of the West had struck. Increasingly the aristocratic East was yielding leadership to it. Andrew Jackson was president. The march of settlers for the Mississippi River and the Pacific Ocean was in full swing. Railroads were just beginning to reach out bands of steel toward the farthest outposts. A system of public schools was taking shape. America—big, uncoordinated, and self-conscious as an adolescent boy—was coming of age.

Robert Richardson was now in his twenty-eighth year. As we have seen, he had been writing for Walter Scott's *Evangelist* for some time, having divided his compositions between it and Alexander Campbell's *Millennial Harbinger*. The *Evangelist* was run on a shoestring, for Walter Scott was poor. His impulsive generosity kept him that way. He therefore had nothing upon which to rely for the conduct of the magazine but the income from subscriptions. These were always in arrears. This meant that the editorial assistant had to work gratis, supporting himself by his medical practice. The young doctor did not complain, for he had expected it to be that way.

Identifying himself with the cause of the Disciples still more intimately was deeply satisfying to him, but this identification was kept as a private pleasure. No change in the masthead, announcing him as assistant editor, was made, nor did the magazine anywhere carry notice of his coming. He did not even sign his articles by his own name. Occasionally he affixed the unrevealing initials, "R. R." or simply "R." But most generally he wrote for this publication under three separate pen names: "Silas," "Alumnus" and "Discipulus." Thus he was able to preserve his anonymity and to assume an unobtrusive role in strong support of one of the main actors in the drama of the reformation, without drawing undue attention to himself.

Over these various pen names and initials, he contributed a stream of articles to this magazine: two articles on "Christian Decorum," two on the "Kingdom of Heaven," two on "Thoughts on Parables," three on the interpretation of Scripture under the title "Simplification," one on "Eternal Life," and another "Faith Comes by Hearing." These appeared during 1834 and 1835. In addition, he proofread each issue and prepared manuscripts for the press. The old spelling and typographical errors which appeared so often while Scott was editing this publication alone, now vanished as if by magic. The doctor had painfully weak and troublesome eyes, but this did not prevent him from seeing details which the other missed.

In his essays on "Simplification"[1] he warned against two extremes of biblical interpretation, the extreme of "mystification" on the one hand, and "the error of *simplifying the religion of Jesus Christ so far as to destroy its identity*" on the other. If the Calvinists inclined toward the first extreme, the Disciples were in danger of being caught in the second. It required some art to understand the Scriptures, and there were laws of biblical interpretation to be learned.

> Indeed, the beauty, the uses, and the characteristic properties of everything is destroyed by too remote an analysis. The blooming rose with all its charms, may be changed into the same simple elements as the poisonous hemlock; and the brilliant diamond which glitters upon the tiara, may be converted into charcoal.

The doctor was already beginning to detect and to warn against the dangers of a mechanical legalism in the new religious movement. He even embellished his article with a touch of humor, saying that "those who are so *fond of simplicity, show much simplicity themselves.*"

The pen of "R. R." illumined all that it touched. It probed more deeply than most, finding hidden or unsuspected corners of thought, and at the same time it never forgot that it was dealing with Christianity as a living body of truth, an organism within which there was a heartbeat of the spirit. Yielding neither to uncontrolled mysticism, nor to unimaginative legalism, he strove to disclose Christianity as life rather than dogma and to reveal the church as a movement more than an institution.

What he wrote delighted the senior editor, but it interested Alexander Campbell even more. This watchful eye of the reformation saw that Robert Richardson was no common scribbler, adding nothing more than volume to the growing periodical literature of the Disciples. His insights were illuminating and fertile with suggestions. In particular, the editor of the *Millennial Harbinger* was struck by Alumnus' two "Thoughts on Parables."[2] In the course of the second of these two articles, their author had taken notice of the phrase "Kingdom of Heaven," which had previously been supposed to signify the *Church*. Dr. Richardson believed this oversimplification to be endlessly confusing because it made nonsense of many passages of Scripture. He showed, therefore, that "the idea involved in 'kingdom' was a compound one, embracing at least three distinct conceptions—viz., a *king*, *subjects*, and the *territory* or place where the subjects lived under the government of their king. In the kingdom of heaven Jesus was the *king*, those who had acknowledged him were the *subjects*, and the world [*kosmos*] in which they lived was the *territory*."

Reporting much later on the influence of his ideas concerning the kingdom, Richardson observed, "This view both Mr. Campbell and Mr. Scott regarded as an important addition to the truths developed during the progress of the Reformation."[3]

Soon adopting the idea as his own, Mr. Campbell fell to work elucidating it in an extra of the *Millennial Harbinger* on "The Kingdom of Heaven." This was published in August, 1834.[4]

It was to be expected that both Robert and Rebekah would become intimately involved in the life of the Carthage church. The doctor was soon chosen clerk of this organization, and in November, 1834, was made one of a committee—with Solomon Rodgers, John Ludlow, Harvey Fairchild, William Myers, and Hezekiah Wood —which was "to take charge of the government and edification of the meeting" and "to hear and examine into all cases of discipline, to prepare them for the consideration of the church when it becomes necessary to make them public, and so to manage and arrange them that the laws of Christ shall be faithfully executed and unity, peace, and love be preserved among the Brethren."[5] The Carthage church records of November 29, 1835, show that the young doctor was a trusted leader, for these minutes resolved "that there be appointed to teach . . . B. U. Watkins, Robert Richardson, Walter Scott."

In the spring of 1835, while on his tour of southern Ohio, Indiana, and Kentucky, Alexander Campbell came out from Cincinnati to visit Walter Scott and Robert Richardson. He found the Richardson family cozy and happy. Nathaniel was now more than two years old, and a baby sister, Anne, was born May 13, 1835.[6]

It was now six years since the Campbell-Owen debate. It was more than three years since the movements of Stone and Campbell had united. The brotherhood numbered possibly 30,000 at this time and was spreading at such a rapid pace that Walter Scott's vision of winning over the whole world did not seem wholly visionary. Alexander Campbell himself had by now attained a very considerable celebrity, far wider than the brotherhood itself. His debates and his magazines were chiefly responsible for this. Besides, he was an impressive personality, a man upon whom the mantle of greatness seemed to rest.

The effect of this visit was to deepen a resolution that had been growing in the young doctor's mind. For some time he had felt that he was doing too little for the cause. He wanted to surrender his full time to it and was determined to do so even if it meant living on the edge of poverty. The more he thought of it, the more certain he became regarding the course he should pursue. Accordingly, in late November or early December, 1835, he wrote to Alexander Campbell, offering to devote his "whole energies to the work of the Lord, on prospect of only a reasonable earthly support." He went on to suggest that he might even go as an evangelist to France. His fluency in the French tongue fitted him for just such an assignment!

When Alexander Campbell replied, he was delighted with the offer of Robert Richardson's services, but, he said, "Touching the tour to France, and the desire you have expressed of introducing the gospel as formerly preached in that country, I cannot speak with much confidence of my own readiness."[7] He went on to say that he was not sure as to what kind of public speaker the doctor was:

> I have never been favored with hearing one discourse from you to a popular assembly either in French or English. I have heard you speak a little in a church on some points of order or of doctrine, and converse by the social hearth but further than this deponent saith not. As I hear, I judge.

Campbell then suggested that since Richardson had never done much evangelistic work, it might be best to try out his talents in his native land for some two or three years before making plans to go abroad. Campbell hastened to explain, however, that he really had something entirely different in mind for the doctor:

> I have, indeed, for some two or three years often thought of visiting the land of my fathers, England, Scotland, Ireland and if the Lord opened the way, I have been willing to make preparation and to spend a year or two in those countries. . . .
>
> Now, if it could be so arranged that you would accompany me to England, or in case it should be thought by both of us to be more eligible for you to attend to my office of editor in my absence, or that after my return you should go to France *via* England, I should think that we had done our immediate duty, and that our anticipations of the spread and progress of the truth might be greatly enlarged as respects Europe.

So! Mr. Campbell thought highly enough of him to propose that he, a young fledgling, should occupy his editorial chair in the senior editor's absence! Here was a proposal that looked even better than his own suggestion of evangelizing France.

In any case, Mr. Campbell went on to say, he had a definite proposal to make for the present:

> As preparatory to this prospect, as necessary to our present obligations and prospects at home, I will make you the following proposition:
>
> Come to Bethany next April. I will find you a comfortable little *wigwam* which I have built since you were here (a frame building one story, containing three apartments on one floor 30 feet in front by 10 in width, having under the same roof a folding room for Harbinger) and I will guarantee you five hundred dollars for the year. I may want your assistance and supervision of the affairs of the press for a part of your time, say

three or four months of the year while I may be absent on some tours, but that need not much interfere with your labors in the word.

Reading this letter with mounting excitement, Robert and Rebekah exchanged happy glances over the words:

There will be a garden connected with the house. I have rented almost all my premises to E. Bakewell from whom you can find pasture for a horse and cow. I need not be further particular. You will freely and familiarly communicate all your views on these points as soon as possible.

Alexander Campbell's proposal brought joy to both Robert and Rebekah. After all, Bethany was in the same county with Wellsburg, and Rebekah would be close to her home place. In addition to a more vital role in the reformation, the prospect of living in Bethany itself, and of working almost daily with the acknowledged leader of the reformation, filled him with exquisite delight.

Just a little earlier, he had written the editor of the *Millennial Harbinger* a long letter in which, among other things, he had said: "Fancy, annihilating time and space, renews the pleasures of the past, presenting again to me your hospitable mansion embosomed by lofty hills which shield it from the storm, permitting me once more to partake with the social circle around the cheerful hearth in happy and solemn conversation respecting the high matters of our holy religion, the love of Christ, the restoration of the gospel, and the salvation of the world."[8]

Now, it would be no longer necessary to visit that hospitable Bethany fireside in fancy—it could be done in fact. The doctor had already disclosed himself from behind the mask of his various pseudonyms to the readers of the *Millennial Harbinger*. At the close of an article in which he had written somewhat bluntly about the abuses of the press in some quarters of the brotherhood, he said that he thought it proper, after such "plainness of speech," to drop the signatures of *Discipulus* and *Alumnus*, and sign his own name to this article and to those he expected to write in the future.[9]

He was going to his new work, the fledgling editor said, with a strong conviction about its worth. "The press is indeed a mighty engine," he said, "and stands pre-eminent among the means by which the Truth has been disseminated." In fact, the prospect of his new work was so pleasing to him that the physician could not wait until April to move to Bethany. The records of the Carthage church read: "February 14, 1836. Brother Richardson, being about to move away and having resigned his appointment as clerk of the society, the Church appointed Brother John Ludlow to fill his place." Early in March he was located in Bethany, soon enough, in fact, to serve as secretary of "the Churches of Christ in co-operation in the Western District of Virginia," meeting in Wheeling on March 19.[10] Richardson was the "eternal" secretary; wherever he went, he was clerk of the meeting; and whenever committees were appointed, he was on them!

Robert Richardson had much to contribute to Alexander Campbell. One of the Disciples of the second generation who knew both men, said:

He was especially a fine critic. His scientific studies were helpful to him in forming exact conclusions with respect to

Biblical interpretation, and nowhere perhaps did he manifest greater ability than in the field of Biblical exegesis. It was here that he was a great helper to Mr. Campbell. The latter's fondness for generalization sometimes led him into doubtful statements with respect to particular things. Not so with Dr. Richardson. He was careful about the most minute matters, and while many of his criticisms and Biblical interpretations had upon them the stamp of originality, he never, in a single instance, advocated any position which may not be defended on purely critical grounds. Indeed, it is well known to a few who are still living that he saved Mr. Campbell from some critical mistakes which the latter would have made had it not been for his trustworthy and able co-labourer.[11]

CHAPTER VI

BETHANY "WIGWAM"

It was March, 1836, when Robert and Rebekah Richardson moved into Alexander Campbell's "cozy wigwam" with two-year-old Nathaniel and ten-month-old Anne. Early that same month, almost unimaginably far to the west in this boundless American continent, Texas revolted against Mexico, and at San Antonio the Alamo defenders were wiped out to a man. The country, without knowing it, was on the verge of an economic depression. Whittier, the New England poet and abolitionist, was singing his songs; and Washington Irving was writing his fanciful tales of the Catskills. With the admission of Arkansas to the Union in this same year, the United States of America now numbered twenty-five.

The "wigwam," which Alexander Campbell had built since 1834 and to which he had invited the Richardsons, was a three-room log cabin on the banks of Buffalo Creek, not more than two hundred yards east of Campbell's own residence. The cabin faced away from the creek, and each of its three rooms had a separate front entrance; while in the rear a small lean-to served as the folding room for the *Millennial Harbinger*.

Flowing past their house, the Buffalo wound its way through wooded hills, twenty-six serpentine miles to Wellsburg, whereas a man on horseback traveled only seven to reach that river town. A turnpike road, stretching sixteen miles across the hills between Bethany and Wheeling, was the only highway.

The Campbell farm, including the present village of Bethany, lay within two giant coils of the creek, describing a letter "S" about one mile across. Near the bottom of the lower coil were located Campbell's home, his solitary study, his printing rooms, and the post office, as well as the Richardson home. The top coil described the town limits of Bethany village and the hill known as "Point Breeze." At this date, the village was no more than a suggestion of a town, with a few log cabins and two or three brick houses and a stone church. About midway in the swing of the Buffalo's letter "S" stood a flour mill, powered by water from a millrace in the stream, and below that, on the side toward the "mansion," nestled the miller's cabin. A road, like the vertical stroke of a dollar sign, ran from one end of the "S" to the other, from the "mansion" to Point Breeze. Lining this road on either side, Mr. Campbell had planted an unbroken avenue of locust trees, which soon imparted their name to the brief stretch of road, thereafter known as "Locust Lane." The natural beauty of Bethany was to the Richardsons a thing of wonder and of joy.

If Dr. Richardson had come to Bethany expecting to abandon his role of physician, he had been mistaken. He was living too close to Wellsburg and to many of his former patients for that. Very soon he began to be called by his neighbors when members of their families became ill. In a short time he was giving himself both to his work as editor and as a family physician, serving a wide community. The doctor on horseback once again rode along the streams and over the hills of Brooke County. From this time on, however, like Luke the physician, who was

a companion and fellow laborer of the Apostle Paul, the
Bethany doctor subordinated his medical profession to his
religious activities.

Alexander Campbell had needed an assistant for some
time. His frequent and protracted absences from his editorial desk not only made his work as a publisher burden-
some; it also prevented his close attention to a voluminous
correspondence. Ample secretarial assistance he already
had, and he did not need simply another amanuensis. He
needed someone who could be trusted to work out details
after the main outlines of a task had been sketched, someone who could relieve him of a large part of his correspondence by assuming direct responsibility for conducting
it according to his own judgment. This called for teamwork of an unusual quality, and he counted on finding it
in Robert Richardson.

The Bethany editor began to rely upon that teamwork
at once. He planned a tour of Northeastern America
which would take him away from home and office during
all the late spring, summer, and early fall of 1836. To
the readers of his magazine he announced: "Meanwhile,
the Press at home will be conducted by our much esteemed
and beloved brother, Dr. *Robert Richardson*, whose abili-
ties for this work may easily be inferred from his various
communications in the volumes of the Harbinger." At
the same time, he apologized for neglecting his correspondence and then pointed out that Dr. Richardson's
coming to Bethany now enabled him to promise prompter
attention:

All letters containing *queries, difficulties,* . . . or *disciplinary* matters, are, during my absence, to be attended to by him. From these letters, which require the attention of the public or of particular churches, he will write such essays as will engross these matters; or he will directly reply to them, according to the wisdom given to him.[1]

In becoming temporary manager of the famed *Millennial Harbinger*, the physician-editor shared the field with nine other reformation periodicals. Besides Walter Scott's *Evangelist*, there were Barton W. Stone's *Christian Messenger*, now published in Jacksonville, Illinois; Dr. John Thomas' *Apostolic Advocate*, of Richmond, Virginia; the *Gospel Advocate*, edited by J. T. Johnson and Alexander Hall, of Georgetown, Kentucky; Silas E. Shepherd's *Primitive Christian*, issued from Auburn, New York; the *Christian Investigator*, edited in Eastport, Maine, by William Hunter; the *Christian Preacher*, D. S. Burnet, Cincinnati, editor; the *Christian Reformer*, John R. Howard, of Paris, Tennessee, editor; and the *Disciple*, of Alabama, with Butler and Graham as editors.[2]

There was much in some of these magazines that was controversial, even in bad taste, but nothing could stop the multiplying of journals, although none of them lived very long. Their presence, however, stirred up the reading public and served to keep the new editor on tiptoes.

These "queries" and "difficulties" the junior editor now handled with deft skill. By way of illustration, we snatch a few fragments out of some of these replies:

"By what *law* would you convince a man that he was a *sinner*, who had never heard of, nor read Old Testament or New?" asked a correspondent of the Cherokee Nation,

Louisiana. *"Upon their own principles* and *by their own reasonings,"* Robert Richardson replied, adding, "See Paul's discourse at Athens and at Lystra."[3]

Is it right to hold the Lord's Supper without a minister? asked someone from Pennsylvania. All Christians are ministers, the doctor replied.

"The subject of Creeds is before me," another questioner began. "I do doubt the utility of them. Still some doubts prevail. . . . If we adopt no formula or creed but the New Testament, how shall we escape the Unitarian, Universalist, &c.? These sects *profess* to be governed by the Sacred Oracles." The real question here, said the junior editor in a lengthy reply, was whether the Scriptures are plain. "We say that if the Scriptures are subjected to the same established rules of interpretation according to which *all other* books and writings are understood, that the true meaning of them can be distinctly and definitely ascertained, and that the true meaning is the only meaning." But if we are to arrive at this true meaning, he went on to explain, we must come to the Bible to be taught by it rather than to make it serve us with texts that prove our dogmas and support our prejudices.[4]

A strict "Independent," concerned over certain trends toward cooperation which he had witnessed in the growing reformation, wrote to protest that it was "a departure from the simplicity of the Christian institution to have cooperation meetings with *Presidents* and *Secretaries,* calling for the *Messengers* of churches, and laying off districts." Where, he wanted to know, was the scriptural warrant for these titles and organizations? In an extended reply, Dr. Richardson said, "A thing may be *un*scriptural, but it does not therefore follow that it is *anti*-scriptural." It does not become so until it is imposed as a term of communion. The rule of church life is that we should do what is natural and simple. When we look at our religion, we see in it many necessary items not covered by Scripture, such as church buildings and orders of service. The same holds in the theological field. Christians entertain various opinions that are unscriptural which are not necessarily antiscriptural, so long as they are simply held as private opinions. "If, however, they should attempt to impose them upon each other, or make them a term of communion, this would indeed be *anti*-scriptural, since we are commanded to receive one another without regard to differences of opinion."[5]

Many other "queries" were answered through the pages of the *Harbinger*; not a few others were dealt with directly. The portion of Mr. Campbell's correspondence falling to "R. R." was voluminous.

Editor Richardson in the first year of his new position also planned and wrote a series of seven articles on the providence of God. The providence of God, he said, is "the care of God in the preservation and government of the world." Both creation and miracles are excluded from the doctrine of providence. "The creating of Adam . . . displayed as much power as would be exhibited in raising a man from the dead—but not any more than is required to clothe the little germ contained in a grain of corn with a *new body*, twelve or fourteen feet high, with its tassel, its silk, its ears, and its shining leaves." The world is a perpetual, orderly miracle. "There is nothing more conducive to the happiness as well as the safety of the Christian, than to encourage himself in a constant dependence upon God, 'who giveth us all things richly to enjoy.'" In such an atmosphere, prayer is natural, more especially since God governs all, but gives special care to some, namely, those who put their trust in him. "May we not indeed say that an abiding sense of the superintending care of God is the test of a standing or falling Christian?"

It was probably in this year that Dr. Richardson formed the habit of carrying a notebook with him everywhere he went. This little pocket-sized book became his paper memory. In it he entered everything he wanted to remember, from a grocery list to a sublime idea. These items were entered as they came to him, while he was writing, walking, reading, or traveling. He called the little leather-bound friend his "Common-place book." From time to time parargaphs from the "Common-place book" appeared in the *Harbinger* to delight or stimulate the readers. Here were telling words about clarity in a speaker: "People are wont to admire a speaker who uses high flowing words above their comprehension. They think the stream is deep because they cannot see the bottom, and do not consider that it is owing to its *muddiness*."[6]

Although Alexander Campbell's printing establishment was the scene of a very considerable publishing business, even beyond the Bethany editor's own writings and magazines, Robert Richardson did not now concern himself with the mechanical side of it. Indeed, he never did learn anything about the techniques of printing. He was busy enough with its editorial side.

He kept up a constant correspondence with the senior editor, following him on his 1836 tour through New York and New England. On August 8 of this year, Campbell wrote Richardson a long letter from Boston, in which he dealt with many points about which the doctor had written him:[7]

> I have felt so exhausted that I dare not speak much in these cities, the air not being very favorable at this season to much energy. I prefer the village and hamlet.
>
> I opened and read in order the immense mail which had for three weeks been accumulating here, upon the perusal of which I was upon the whole, much refreshed. It was nearly three weeks since I heard anything from home.

The Bethany sage then commended his junior editor for the excellent way in which he was conducting matters in the senior editor's absence. Mr. Campbell especially praised an essay on "Inspiration of the Scriptures" which the young coeditor had written for the *Harbinger*. "It is a cardinal thought that you have hit upon in that essay," he declared.

Needless to say, this commendation of his article delighted young Richardson immensely. In it he had undertaken to show that one of the proofs of the inspiration of the Bible was that it dealt, not with the easily perverted function of allaying curiosity, but with that of giving practical guidance to man's moral and spiritual life on this earth. He was somewhat acid in his remarks about those who looked in Holy Writ for such things as the secret cause of Satan's expulsion from heaven, observing that "such knowledge might be of use to devils, but it cannot profit man." Regarding the Bible as a disclosure of information about the supernatural realm was, in fact, the pernicious cause of much of the strife then agitating the denominations. A healthier view was needed:

> And it is with me a consideration of no little weight as it regards the proof of the inspiration of the sacred volume, that *it is the only professed revelation of spiritual and eternal things which is free from* EVERY THING CALCULATED TO GRATIFY MERELY A VAIN CURIOSITY. . . . It gives us no useless history of devils or of angels—the secret counsels of eternity remain undisclosed—the peculiar condition of departed spirits is not detailed—nor are the inhabitants of the sun, moon, and stars described. It is intended for man during his abode upon this earth. . . . It is designed to elevate and perfect the character of man. . . . Nothing whatever is introduced which has no tendency to inspire confidence, fortitude, and hope, or lead to personal purity and practical benevolence.[8]

Yes, reflected Robert, he was glad that his senior editor agreed with this "cardinal thought." He returned to his reading of the letter, in the closing paragraphs of which, Alexander Campbell again brought up the matter of his physical exhaustion, reluctantly admitting that he had finally reached the stage where he "must taper off." Informing Richardson that he would be back in Bethany the first week in September, he brought the letter to a close.

The collaboration of Richardson and Campbell in these months of 1836 foreshadowed what was later fully sustained: they made a good team. Campbell was a great student of the arts and religion, a powerful religious statesman with real sagacity, while Robert Richardson was a keen student of science and religion, a quiet thinker, and a retiring but firm adviser. Both recognized that they worked well together. One was the advocate, while the other was the counselor. Their cooperation was not a result of sameness; it was, rather, a harmony of difference. One was coldly intellectual; the other was warmly devotional, almost mystical. In fact, as one of Campbell's biographers said, "with his peculiar temperament he [Richardson] was always more nearly a mystic than any other of the pioneer Disciples."[9]

One was quickly depressed by too many details; the other mastered them easily:

> It was just here where Dr. Richardson was of supreme value to him [Mr. Campbell]. While he and Mr. Campbell would often talk over in a general way the chief points to be considered, it was finally left to Dr. Richardson to work out the details and to make a decision in the case. His judgment was scarcely ever at fault, and his patience in pursuing a subject to the last analysis made his conclusions almost infallible with respect to everything he investigated. He never stopped with the surface of things, but made his examination thorough, so that nothing was left to be considered.[10]

As this team worked on into the closing months of the year, the first seven years of the *Millennial Harbinger* were completed. This was exactly the number of years that the *Christian Baptist* had lived; so the *Harbinger* to this point was called the "first series." The senior editor informed his readers: "Encouraged . . . by an improvement in my health, and by the able assistance of our accomplished brother Dr. R. RICHARDSON, I have resolved to commence (the Lord willing) a *new series* of the *Millennial Harbinger* after the close of the present volume."[11]

It was just at this juncture, however, that Robert Richardson's eyes went on strike again. Bathing them failed to bring the expected relief. After a while it became plain that nothing would restore them but a complete rest from reading and writing. The doctor decided to turn his misfortune to advantage. While resting his eyes he would make an excursion into the field to promote the sale of the *Millennial Harbinger* and to lend such other aid to the cause of the reformation as opportunity might afford. On June 9, 1837, he left for Kentucky.[12] His faithful horse, Barney, provided transportation. In a trip extending to August 18, he visited Lancaster, Tarleton, Chillicothe, and Middletown in Ohio, and Georgetown, Maysville, Paris, Stanford, Lexington, and Mays Lick in Kentucky. As a student of nature, he especially enjoyed the fields, the woods, the farmhouses, the orchards, and the fine cattle which he saw in the valleys of the Muskingum and Scioto rivers.

From Maysville, Kentucky, he dictated a long letter to Alexander Campbell regarding his excursion, in which he dropped a few items of a personal nature. In particular, he mentioned that the trouble with his eyes, which had induced him to leave his work at Bethany to make this trip, was somewhat relieved. Recovery, however, was far from complete, and it was still necessary to avail himself of "the aid of an amanuensis."

From Nicholasville, Kentucky, he wrote Rebekah on July 26, 1837:

I arrived at this place a week ago and having received no news from home since I started, proceeded to Lexington where I had the happiness to receive a letter from you and one also from

Bro. Campbell. I thank the Lord that he has preserved you all in peace and prosperity. I met Bro. Scott (for the first time since leaving home) in Lexington, and heard from him that they are doing well at Carthage. . . . I have delayed a few days longer in order to settle if possible the dissensions in the church here. A few years ago there was a church here of about 200 members apparently in a flourishing condition. For the last 3 years, however, they have been constantly quarreling, and the members meeting latterly have been only 10 or 15. There have been three parties and the whole neighborhood has been torn by their contentions so that they had become a byword and reproach. I have succeeded, after laboring for several days among them, in public and from house to house, in effecting an entire settlement of their difficulties and a perfect reconciliation between all parties.

He went on to say that at the meeting at which peace was finally restored, the whole congregation was in tears. The day on which the letter was being written had been set aside by the church for fasting and prayer. Richardson then brought the letter to a close with these paragraphs:

I am now at the house of Father Simms who is a fine intelligent and hospitable disciple. I expect to set out tomorrow for Mortonsville and Versailles at the last of which places a three days' meeting commences on Friday. I have concluded not to go to Louisville at present as it will keep me too long from home. I have been very much afflicted with the dyspepsia for the last ten days.

I have met with many devoted and intelligent disciples in Kentucky. I am much pleased with Sister Forbes of Stanford. She is the most intelligent female I have found in any of the churches here. Sister Dodd of Lancaster . . . is also a fine disciple.

Tell Nathl. and Anne that I will come home again after a while. I long to see you all. The Lord bless you.

At Mays Lick, he had seen and heard the eloquent J. T. Johnson, former United States congressman, and now an untiring evangelist of the cause. "He conquers opposition by the force of his zeal," he reported, "or disarms it by the warmth of his benevolence. And so evident is his sincerity and philanthropy, that, while others by *reasoning* move the *heads* of the audience, he touches their *hearts* with his *own heart.*"[13]

He brought his visit to a close. Taking the steamer at Maysville, he docked at Wellsburg and rode on to Bethany, arriving home on August 18, 1837. He had been gone a little more than two months, but his eyes were not yet equal to editorial work. He was forced to support himself almost wholly by his medical practice, and he had to keep away from the books and papers which he loved so well.

In the fall of this same year—October 12, 1837, to be exact—a third child was born. She was named Julia, for Richardson's mother. The little log cabin, with its three small rooms, was becoming crowded.

Throughout the whole of the next year, he was able to read or write so little that he contributed only two or three articles to the *Harbinger*. At the end of 1838, Alexander Campbell wrote, somewhat sadly:

> Brother Richardson having, from the weakness of his eyes, been constrained to give up, in a great measure, both reading and writing, has, for the present volume, been unable to render me any essential assistance. Should his eyes continue to improve, he will furnish one or two articles per number for the next volume.[14]

Unwilling to be idle in the work of reform, he bundled Rebekah off to her folks at Wheeling and left for an

Eastern tour in the early months of the year 1838. He was absent for several weeks, visiting such cities as York-town and Baltimore.

Back in Bethany, working at his medical practice, and waiting for his eyes to return to normal, Robert Richardson's mind was busy with the future. Although he was regaining his sight, almost certainly the attack would be renewed when he least expected it. Besides, their present home would not long accommodate a growing family. It was imperative that more adequate shelter and a more dependable income should be provided for his loved ones. Considering again his misfortunes, but not complaining, he studied them to see how they could be turned to advantage.

Chapter VII

BETHPHAGE, "NIGH UNTO BETHANY"

Toward the end of 1838 the tormented physician found a solution to his problem. He took his clue from Alexander Campbell, who had always run a prosperous farm in connection with his other enterprises. Indeed, it was the Campbell farm that financed many of his ventures, both journalistic and educational. So Robert Richardson also bought a farm.

Since his visit at Ravens Vale twelve years before, a love for the country and farming had possessed him. His association with Campbell had deepened these attachments. And now, he could indulge his longings on his own account.

The farm he purchased was small—nothing like the thousands of acres held by Campbell. In fact, it was only a little over sixty-seven acres, nestling in the slight depression of a hatlike hill, looking down upon Bethany from across the Buffalo. It was reached by road past Point Breeze on the Bethany-Wheeling turnpike, two miles away from the village. The farm itself was situated back from the road, out of sight from the highway. The depression which formed this farm was exactly the shape of an outdoor amphitheater. Upon the stage of the amphitheater stood a six-room log cabin. Back of the cabin, the stage fell away into a tangled, wooded hillside which tumbled down several hundred feet to the creek. The eye which looked out across this stage to the scenic hills beyond saw no other human habitation and could be seen from none. The farm was truly an "Arcadian retreat."

Walking from the house up to the ridge to the right, which formed the north wing of the amphitheater, Richardson could look down, across the winding Buffalo, to the village of Bethany and the hills which rose by stages beyond it. The view was clear, and beautiful to the point of enchantment. Such a place could have only one name, for it was "nigh unto Bethany." He would call it "Bethphage." The deed shows that Dr. Richardson bought this farm from Moses and March A. Hedges on March 30, 1839, for the sum of $2,234.17. Of this amount, he was able to raise all but $1,000 in cash. This $1,000 he obtained from Alexander Campbell on a mortgage, to be retired, at regular interest, in four installments, beginning April 1, 1841, and concluding April 1, 1844.

The Richardson family moved into Bethphage immediately, and the doctor fell to work at once, transforming the farm into an orderly pattern. Robert's father, Nathaniel Richardson, came out from Pittsburgh to superintend the planning of the yard and gardens. This he did in the English style. With its summer house, its rose bower, its shrubs and perennial flowers, this garden would shortly become a wilderness of beauty, attracting visitors from afar.

About the farm, the doctor saw to it that stone walls were built to serve as retainers for roads and building approaches. One of these was at the spring, just fifty feet north of the house, and served as a means of holding the bank in place. This spring poured forth an abundant stream of cold, pure water. About it the doctor-farmer built a stone springhouse, with basin and milk trough. He planned the second floor of this building as a shop to house the smaller farm tools.

In time, a weeping willow tree grew by this springhouse. One day early in their life at Bethphage, Rebekah, returning from a horseback ride, took the willow branch which she had been using for a riding whip and thrust it into the ground near the spring. In later years it grew into a weeping willow tree of such giant size that its fame attracted many visitors on its own account.

By this same spring the doctor planted some English water cress, which he greatly enjoyed in a salad. Gradually, the water cress spread, finally finding its way along a rill all the way down to Buffalo Creek. Thence it trailed along the banks for twenty-six miles to the Ohio River, where it spread for several miles downstream.

The doctor built a bank barn on the farm. The first one of its sort in this vicinity, it was equipped with box stalls for the horses and calves and stanchions for the cows, all located in the basement; wheat and oat bins were installed on the first floor, with the second floor serving as a haymow.

Busily he superintended the transforming of a commonplace farm into a garden spot. Orange hedges were planted to fence the fields. In the garden, near the house, berry bushes of all kinds were planted. He started an orchard with pears, cherries, plums, and apples of many varieties: Early Harvest, Rambo, Maiden's Blush, Vandevers, Rhode Island Greening, Yellow Belle Flere, and Winesap! Currant bushes and grapevines were also planted.

In the vegetable garden he raised cabbages, Irish and sweet potatoes, celery, lima beans, and string beans. The doctor believed that proper eating had much to do with health. He taught his family, whose nourishment was to come almost exclusively from this farm, that soil, atmosphere, water, and light are man's great physical friends.

Richardson also saw to it that his farm was well stocked with domestic animals: riding and farm horses, cows, pigs, and sheep. The first summer, he bought hogs: a sow for $6.00, another sow for $10, and a sow and pigs for $6.00. The following year, he bought a cow and a calf for $13 and ten lambs at $1.50 each. By 1846 he had 104 sheep and thirty-eight lambs, and that year his wool crop amounted to 311 pounds. He valued sheep not only because of the mutton and wool which they provided, but also because they were the "avowed enemies" of weeds and underbrush. He could never tolerate a dock or a thistle on the place. When he came across one on his way into or out of the farm, it was his habit to dismount from his horse and pull up the dock or cut out the thistle and carry the weed into the house to burn it in the fireplace.

There was a place for poultry, too. He selected chickens and turkeys of pure breeds but left their care to Rebekah and his hired help. He himself could not endure the cackling of hens! To him it was a most hideous noise.

When he planted his crops it was only after making a chemical analysis of the soil. He studied farm journals and books to find out which crops were most suitable to his part of the country. He also introduced some new ones, including Fultz wheat. Although this virgin land was so fertile that it would produce fairly well with no attention, he had no intention of mining out its riches and impoverishing the soil. He fertilized the ground and rotated the crops. He had great respect for clover, of which he grew a field every year, but in a different place. In this first year, he invested $10 in limekilns— an indication that he began his farming with a wholesome respect for the soil.

Robert Richardson's earlier life of affluence in Pittsburgh having accustomed him to the use of servants, he encouraged Rebekah to get a maid to help her with the house and children. She employed "a certain maiden who contracted to help with the work" at 50 cents a week, but in that same summer, 1839, a different young woman had to be employed at 62½ cents a week, the first having resigned. She later returned as a second helper in the house, in 1843, at an increase in wages to 75 cents a week!

For the farm work itself that first year, the doctor hired a single young man at $12 a month. He proved rather unreliable, however, and the following year his job was given to another young man. The new man began his work in January, with the understanding that he was to receive $9.00 a month and was to pay 50 cents a month for washing and mending. Later the contract was changed so that he received $8.00 a month and washing and was allowed to work for other farmers for two weeks at harvest time and thus earn extra wages. By 1841 the work of the farm had grown to the point where two hired hands were required—"John and Charles." A more stable arrangement was soon effected, however, when the doctor built a tenant house on the place and invited a family to occupy it and help with the manual labor.

Finally, with the family cozily settled and their plans in order, "R. R." turned once again to his writing desk. On May 10, 1839, he informed Alexander Campbell that he was now installed in a new home and that he had named it Bethphage because it was "nigh unto Bethany."[1] The room in which he wrote was the middle one of three at the front of the house on the second floor. It was a small room, about twelve feet square, having a hewn-beam ceiling and an open grate. "Its walls were lined with books and even the ceiling was loaded with pamphlets and periodicals which were stuffed in between the exposed joists wherever the cross braces would hold them."[2] On the shelves, "books, papers, sermons, diaries and manuscripts were carefully assorted and labelled. . . . Some shelves were marked: 'Inventions, Schools, Medical, Periodical Literature.' "[3]

This study was his own—private. He even carried the coal for its grate and did his own housekeeping here, so that nothing would be disturbed. No one ever invaded this room uninvited, not even a member of the family! For a writing stand he had a table with a portable desk. Like a school desk, it was grooved for pens and pencils. He made his own pens, from personally selected goose quills, and also manufactured his own ink. Legal cap paper was his preferred writing material, and black sand served as a blotter. A single window admitted his only light during the day, and a candle illumed his studies at night.

As he wrote to Alexander Campbell, he reflected with pleasure on the peace of his house. A low room across the hall and under the eaves was his "drying-room," where he prepared his herbs and medicines. The two remaining rooms on that floor, with log walls and beam ceilings, held large four-poster beds. The stairs to the second floor opened at the back of the kitchen, which was at the north end of the house. The kitchen was a log lean-to. Cooking was done at a large open fireplace, on a swinging crane. The large parlor, beneath the study, was wainscoted in black walnut. It was furnished in antique mahogany furniture, most of which his father had given him: a piano, two tables, a couch, a number of comfortable chairs, and a stately bookcase for the general library of the family. On warm evenings his family visited or received friends on the large front porch, running the length of the house.

The house was heated in the winter by open grates burning coal, which cost 4 cents a bushel. A large, well-appointed cellar under the house was ready for the storing of fruit, potatoes, cabbages, and other vegetables.

With his eyes recovered from their "amaurosis," and his heart gladdened under a comfortable roof, Robert Richardson unlimbered his quill pen in this year of 1839 to write a few articles for the *Millennial Harbinger*. There was a series of six on "Sin—A Dialogue," another series of six articles on "The Gospel," and a number of incidental pieces.

It was also in this first year at Bethphage that the Richardson family rejoiced over the birth of a fourth child, a girl, on October 31, 1839. Robert and Rebekah named her Mary. Nathaniel was now nearly seven, Anne was four and a half, Julia was two, while the father and mother were respectively thirty-three and twenty-three.

Meantime, another venture was afoot. It, too, would involve Dr. Richardson. In the October number of the *Millennial Harbinger*, Alexander Campbell published his fourfold plan for "A New Institution."[4] The Disciples now numbered 40,000, and the movement was advancing! It needed an educated leadership. Mr. Campbell proposed to build a college, and he relied on the doctor to help him do it.

Chapter VIII

A NEW INSTITUTION

LIKE everything else that Alexander Campbell did, the doctor observed, his scheme for an educational system was conceived in broad and comprehensive terms so as to include both mind and spirit from childhood to manhood. *The College* was only one of four branches of the "New Institution" which he proposed to build at Bethany. First, there was to be a *Family Institution* where boys under fourteen would receive their elementary schooling, living together under the careful attention of a patron and a matron who would have as much to do with the molding of their morals as of their minds. Next was the college preparatory division, the *School*, under the supervision of professors in the college, but not itself a part of the college. The third branch was the *College*, and the fourth was the *Church*, an institution which would permeate all others, not simply as a school of religious ideas, but as a laboratory of Christian living. "In this institution it will not be the theory of a church—of Bible-reading, Bible-criticism, Bible-lectures—sermons—church order—Christian discipline; but the daily practice of these. This church will be in session seven days every week."[1] The spearhead for the whole plan was the college, where an equal emphasis should be placed on the arts and sciences, where the Bible should be used as a textbook, and where instruction should follow the inductive lines of the Baconian method.

Robert Richardson knew that his friend had entertained the vision of such an institution for several years and that with the unexpected emergence of Bacon College at Georgetown, Kentucky, in 1836, he had postponed it until that school was firmly established and operating successfully.[2] Now, there was no longer any need for delay. Eighteen incorporators of the college were called into session, and the Bethany physician was one of them. Looking around him at the first meeting, he saw such worthies as Alexander Campbell's father, Thomas, and brother-in-law, Matthew McKeever; three sons-in-law, John C. Campbell, Albert G. Ewing, and Robert Y. Henley. In addition to those having family connections with the Campbells, there were the influential Adamson Bentley, of Warren, Ohio, and Samuel Church, of Pittsburgh, who sat with him in this historic session.[3] The purpose of the meeting was to draw up articles of incorporation and to prepare the petition to the legislature of Virginia for a charter. John C. Campbell, formerly a Virginia legislator, and now a prominent Wellsburg attorney, would undertake to present the petition.

To that end, Alexander Campbell and his son-in-law set off for Richmond in February, 1840. When they returned the next month, it was with a charter issued March 2, 1840, which stipulated: "That there be, and is hereby erected and established, at or near Bethany, in the county of Brooke, in this Commonwealth, a Seminary of learning for the instruction of youth in the various branches of science and literature, the useful arts, agriculture, and the learned and foreign languages. . . . *And be it further enacted*, That the said seminary shall be

known and called by the name of Bethany College."
There was to be no "Theological Professorship." This
charter provided for the first official meeting of the
trustees of the new college on the "second Monday in
May next."[4]

Accordingly, on Monday, May 11, 1840, nine trustees,
with the venerable and aged Thomas Campbell in the
chair, met to lay plans for the building of college halls,
the raising of money, the gathering of students, and the
appointment of a faculty. Robert Richardson received
his assignment as a member of the building committee,
to serve along with John C. Campbell, William Stewart,
Matthew McKeever, and Alexander Campbell.[5]

Work was undertaken at once on a kind of hotel and
dormitory to be called "Steward's Inn" and designed to
accommodate a hundred students, and a few occasional
guests. This was built at Alexander Campbell's own expense on a ten-acre campus carved out of his farm on an
"Areopagus" hill which rose above the village of Bethany.
The new campus was located at the extreme right of the
upper coil of the Buffalo's enormous letter "S." Back
of this hill, in turn, and as a continuation of it, rose the
sheltering height of an "Acropolis," which as custodian of
the college water supply, was soon to be known as "Reser-
voir Hill."

When the trustees met again on September 18, they
authorized the building committee "to erect such buildings as they may deem necessary" and to "procure per-
manent furniture, including beds and bedding, for the
building in progress of erection." Mr. Richardson and
his committee decided to build a second structure, just

to the right of Steward's Inn, to be known as the main
College Hall. Carpenters and masons were called, and
the work got under way. It was hoped that gifts of
money toward the "Family House" would make it possible for them to build that structure and get sessions in it
under way by the fall of 1842. In the same meeting
Alexander Campbell was elected president and was requested to propose a curriculum and nominate a faculty
and staff, his recommendation to be submitted to the next
meeting.[6]

Meantime the senior editor of the *Millennial Harbinger* had been publishing essays and news about the "New
Institution" all through the year. Even before the
charter was granted, Philip E. Pendleton, of Virginia,
having seen the original proposal of a new institution in
October, 1839, made a will in which he bequeathed $1,000
upon condition that the school should come into being
within five years after his death.[7] Mr. Pendleton had
died on December 28 of the same year, and on February
23, 1840, notice of the bequest reached Bethany. By the
time of the second annual meeting of the trustees on May
10, 1841, $11,054 had been received in pledges to the
new enterprise, $1,405 of it in cash.[8] The buildings
under progress were to cost about $16,000, of which $10,-
000 was advanced by the president, who was also serving
as treasurer.[9]

In the second annual meeting, President Campbell submitted a curriculum, divided into five schools: Sacred
History, Ancient Languages, Mathematics, Chemistry,
and Natural Philosophy.[10] He would himself take the
first, while Andrew F. Ross, of Ohio, was nominated to

teach languages; Charles Steward, of Kentucky, for mathematics; and W. K. Pendleton, of Virginia, for natural philosophy. The chemistry professor was to be the Bethany physician and coeditor of the *Millennial Harbinger*, Robert Richardson.[11]

Some of Alexander Campbell's editorial enemies were sniping at him through their journals with such remarks as: "O yes! it is designed to build up something!—Mind, he is Treasurer!"[12] This kind of innuendo led Robert Richardson to fly to the president's support with a motion, in the May 10, 1841, meeting that Alexander Campbell as treasurer of Bethany College, file a bond of $15,000 (he had previously given one for $10,000). He also moved that the secretary, as a cross check, be required to keep a special book, listing each contribution and the amount given in each case. It was in this same meeting that Richardson moved that the trustees begin buying the college buildings from Mr. Campbell, the first payment to be made October 1, 1843.[13]

Edwin W. Bakewell, of Virginia, was appointed steward until July 4, 1843. It was "*Unanimously resolved*, That the boarding, lodging, washing, and tuition of a student at Bethany College, shall be one hundred and fifty dollars for the collegiate year . . . and that an entrance fee of ten dollars be required for each new student." Robert Richardson, ever watchful physician and hygienist, moved "That the Bill of Fare for the Steward's Inn shall be the same as that of the University of Virginia." Alexander Campbell, John C. Campbell, and Robert Richardson were made a committee to draft a code of by-laws to be submitted in the next meeting, and the trustees adjourned until October 20, 1841.

This summer the professor-elect of chemistry in Bethany College set out on a tour of Kentucky to recruit students and raise money and support for the new institution. While he rode along, his recent ventures in farming at Bethphage caused his eye to quicken as he surveyed the farms and observed farmers' methods. He was alert to nature as well as to institutions, and to men as well as ideas, as is seen in a letter to Rebekah from New Union, Kentucky, dated August 6, 1841.

DEAR REBEKAH,

Not having heard anything from home since I started I have often felt anxious to know how you and the children have been and how John and Charles are getting along with the affairs of the farm. If you have written, I have not received the letters. Should you write when you receive this, direct the letter to Mayslick [*sic*], Mason Co., Ky.

I hope you have all been well and that the divine favour has been extended to you. Tell Julia that I saw a little girl in Madison Co. just the picture of her, and that I will be home to see her after a while. Tell Anne that I wish her to read her book every day, and get by heart some verses of scripture—the beginning of the sermon on the mount. I want my dear Nathaniel to be attentive and careful of things for me and not to neglect reading every day, and attending the Sunday School. Mary I hope will be able to talk when I get home.

This has been a dry season in Kentucky and the crops have suffered much in some places. I hope there has been no failure in mine and that John and Charles have been able to manage them advantageously. I wish them to save up the young clover as much as they can from being pastured too low.

Jane [the maid?] I hope is contented and doing well—endeavor to have her read the scriptures. I saw James in Madison Co. He is doing well. My health is much better than it was some weeks ago. I will endeavor to be home in the beginning of Sept.

Yours affectionately,

R. RICHARDSON

[P. S.] I write this at the house of Louis Pinkerton. I hold a 2 days meeting near this place tomorrow and next day. Mr. Matthews the teacher who formerly taught at Carthage was here today and started for Harrodsburg where he had the care of the preparatory school of Bacon College. He wished to be remembered to you.

R. R.

The opening of the college was delayed from the expected date of September 1 until November 2 by the uncompleted condition of Steward's Inn. The main college building itself would not be ready for occupancy until the following spring. Meantime, preparations were being made to use the Inn for classes as well as boarding and lodging.

The committee on by-laws, of which Richardson was a member, reported in the fall meeting of the trustees on October 20. These by-laws, which were adopted, carefully delineated the conditions of student and faculty life in the college, which was to open in less than two weeks. Some of the regulations read as follows:

The collegiate year [hereafter] shall commence on the 1st day of September, and terminate on the 4th of July following.

. . . .

Each Professor shall make a monthly report to the President—exhibiting the days and the subject of lectures and examination, and the time occupied by each respectively.

. . . .

The College Hall shall be opened every Lord's day morning for religious worship and instruction, to be performed by respectable ministers of various denominations; and it shall be the duty of all Students to attend worship either there or at some other place.

Rough, frontier conditions tended to persist, as one regulation shows:

No student shall introduce, keep, or use within the precincts of the College, weapons or arms of any kind, or gunpowder, or keep a servant, horse, or dog.

. . . .

Smoking segars, or any other use of tobacco, is at all times strictly forbidden within the College precincts.

There were to be no ten o'clock scholars in this college:

The bell shall be rung every morning throughout the collegiate year at dawn. The Students shall rise at this signal, and assemble in the rooms for general meeting, to attend on worship, at such hour as the Faculty may determine.

. . . .

The dress of the Students shall be uniform and plain—shall be of a dark grey, or black color—at a price not exceeding six dollars a-yard—and the coat shall be made single-breasted, and the collar bound round with braid, and a star worked in black silk on each end of it: Provided, that a Student may be allowed to wear any clothes which he may have had when he matriculated; and in Summer any cheap light garments approved by the Faculty.

It is also recommended by the Trustees that the Kentucky Jeans be selected as the cloth for common wearing apparel.

. . . .

The Steward shall furnish the Students with clean sheets and pillow-cases at least once-a-fortnight, and with clean towels at least twice-a-week.

It shall be the duty of the Steward to have the rooms of the Students well swept and ventilated every day. . . .

. . . .

The Steward shall not furnish luxurious fare to the Students; but the fare shall be plentiful, plain, served neatly, and well dressed—of good and wholesome viands. . . .

The Steward shall furnish boarding, lodging, washing, fuel, and one candle for every two Students till bed hour; also, proper attendance of servants for domestic and menial duties . . . for all of which his compensation shall be one hundred dollars for each Student per collegiate year. The clothes to be washed for each Student shall not exceed nine pieces in Winter, and twelve in Summer, per week.[14]

In this same meeting of the trustees, Robert Richardson was appointed, with William Stewart and J. C. Campbell, on an auditing committee.

A regulation touching faculty salaries made them dependent upon the tuition. Fifty dollars of the $150 collected from each student was earmarked as tuition. From this fund the secretary and janitor of the faculty were to be paid, and the remaining amount was to be divided equally among the professors, the president of the institution counting as two. This made Professor Richardson's salary for the first year about $800.

When college opened November 2, 1841, there were 101 students enrolled, of whom all but twenty-three were from

Virginia and Kentucky.[15] Studying, reciting, and board-ing, all took place in Steward's Inn. President Campbell announced in the January, 1842, *Millennial Harbinger*: "We have already formed more than twenty classes. Of these the first meets at half past 6 in the morning. To form and establish that most healthful and useful habit of rising early, I chose that early hour for my lectures on sacred history, for Bible-readings, and worship." When the president was away from the college on one of his numerous tours, these morning lectures fell to Dr. Richardson.

Professor Richardson rode daily to and from the col-lege on horseback. Despite storms, and even floods, he made these trips without ever being tardy during all the years of his teaching. Buffalo Creek, which he was obliged to ford, often became a furious stream after a heavy rain, necessitating the horse's swimming the swift current with the doctor on his back. This was done so often that his horse became adept at it, always landing the rider safely on the opposite bank, though sometimes a long distance down the swift stream. His teaching schedule kept the doctor at the college during the entire day; often faculty meetings and other delays held him until nearly dark. Each day at the usual time, however, his faithful horse presented himself at the accustomed spot for the trip home. In case his rider was not ready, the steed would sometimes wander away, but would re-appear when the doctor blew the whistle attached to the end of his plaited riding whip.

After his schoolwork for the day was over, the physi-cian made his medical calls. In the evening he worked in the candlelighted study, preparing his class lectures and doing his writing and editorial work. In the busy schedule of his crowded day, nothing was out of place, and no time was lost.

Professor Richardson was an original teacher. Within the limitation of available apparatus, he used laboratory methods. He also enlivened his lectures with frequent sallies of wit, forerunners of which could be seen in his face and eyes several moments in advance of the humor itself. His students thought him "keen" and gave him close and respectful attention.

He kept a very close check on the work being done by his students. His gift for reading men was almost uncanny. Hence, he was able to discern inner traits in his various students; this power made him an illuminating teacher and a helpful counselor. The impatient were guided to mastery, and the timid were given hope. Written lessons, tests, examinations, came frequently. He graded examinations carefully and gave rather low marks. He was exacting but kindly and he demanded, above everything else, that his students be open-minded and thorough.

J. W. McGarvey, who studied under him a little later than the period under notice, said: "As a teacher he was as clear as the ringing of a silver bell, and he often indulged in exquisite flashes of humor. If the students were impressed by Mr. Campbell, they were charmed by Dr. Richardson."[16]

Very early in his teaching career, parents of some of the Bethany students hit upon the idea of sending the funds for their college expenses to Professor Richardson for his personal control. In 1841 his ledger reveals that a certain student from Kentucky entered the college under these conditions. His father placed his entire account in the doctor's hands. Two pages of the ledger reveal the way in which these funds were spent for bed, clothing, ink, books, postage, washing, pocket money, and the like. This type of trust was often imposed upon him. As these unofficial duties increased, the physician of Bethany—who was also coeditor of the *Millennial Harbinger*, farmer of Bethphage, secretary of the faculty, clerk of the Bethany church, and professor of chemistry—discovered that he had taken on another activity, that of bursar to the students of Bethany College.

CHAPTER IX

SPIRITUAL PHYSICS: HEAT AND LIGHT

NOT only did Professor Richardson handle private funds for students; he was also bursar of the institution. In this capacity—which was without title and without pay —he collected tuition and other student fees and from them paid college bills, including the salaries of professors. He discharged these services until September 10, 1842, when he turned over his office and a treasury of $1,485 to William K. Pendleton, who was then appointed bursar, with both title and pay. As remuneration for his services, Mr. Pendleton began immediately to collect 1 per cent of all fees handled.[1]

Pendleton was the son-in-law of Alexander Campbell, having married his daughter Lavinia the previous year. Affable and polished in exterior, a true "Southern gentleman," he achieved through his charm more recognition, and certainly more pay, than Richardson could command by painstaking effort. The doctor's patience and thoroughness worked to his own disadvantage. He was the victim of them himself, never being able to slight a task or take a shallow view of anything; and he was victimized by others, who took his quiet accuracy for granted, seldom bothering to acknowledge his services.

By July of 1842 the college was thriving. Treasurer Campbell reported pledges totaling $17,688.25, of which $7,923.66 had been received in cash.[2] There were now 156 students in attendance,[3] the president having announced in the March *Harbinger* that work on the main college building was nearing completion, so that recitation rooms for a larger number of students would be ready about the first of April.[4]

In consequence of his having been elected to the faculty, Professor Richardson resigned his post on the Board of Trustees at the end of this first year.[5]

As teacher of physical science, the doctor began at once to accumulate a laboratory or "museum," as it was called, so as to illustrate the laws of nature set forth by the text-books and the lectures. Although it was not possible then to supply every student with the elaborate equipment for personal experimentation which was later to be standard in all good high schools and colleges, he was able to use the method of lecture-demonstration. With that in view, for the very first session he had purchased bottles, chemicals, drugs, tubes, corks, mortars and pestles, spatulas, and other items of like nature. His published pleas for apparatus met a response from many quarters, so that he was able to acknowledge gifts of philosophical apparatus from P. S. Fall of Kentucky, specimens from the marl beds of eastern Virginia, contributed by John Richardson of that area, and a box of museum curiosities from J. W. Parrish of Woodford County, Kentucky.[6]

Beginning in the fall of 1843, he was teaching chemistry, French, and physiology. This last course is somewhat ornamentally presented in the college catalogue for that year:

> Extra to the usual course of instruction in colleges, lectures were delivered to all the Students on the Anatomy and Physiology of the human system by Professor Richardson without extra

charge. Anatomical preparations adapted to such a course of in-struction having been purchased, so much of these branches of useful sciences as are necessary to the knowledge of 'one's own self' and in order to the intelligent and practical application of the laws of hygiene, can be communicated to all those capable of studying the grammar of any language, ancient or modern.[7]

The doctor's knowledge of ancient languages and his broad culture also fitted him to design the college seal. He worked at this during the early months of the second term, emerging with a seal in which two human figures, representing Science and Truth, were made central. One, holding a quiver of arrows, was receiving a bow from the other. The motto, emblazoned over these figures, read: *"Pharetram Veritas, sed arcum Scientia donat"* ("Truth bears the quiver, but Science gives it the bow").[8]

When Commencement Day for 1843 came around on July 4, so great and so favorable had been the public notice of Bethany College that a horde of 1,500 people poured into the tiny village to attend the exercises. Beginning at 9:30 in the morning, these exercises continued for five hours, without intermission. This protracted meeting was endured, even enjoyed, by those who attended, the enjoyment deriving from the atmosphere of success which enveloped it.[9]

"It is but three years since the first brick was moulded for the erection of Bethany College," its president triumphantly announced. "During this time a College Proper, four stories, 83 by 45; a Steward's Inn, equal to 107 feet by 36, 4 stories; and one wing of a Mansion House, 73 feet by 24, two stories—have been completed." The announcement went on to say:

Connected with the College, though not upon the grounds, a spacious new building has just been erected, which will be ready to receive the primary department at the commencement of next session. Besides the College Common Hall, a Room of 80 by 42 in the clear, and two Society Class Rooms, large enough for 100 students each, there are for the accommodation of Students some 75 or 80 Rooms furnished, affording ample accommodations for 150 or 160 Students within the College precincts. Two Literary Societies have been formed with the nucleus of two Libraries. An incipient College Library and considerable Chemical and Philosophical Apparatus have been procured. The whole subscriptions to this Institution amount to about $25,000.[10]

Thus the initial step in the plan for a fourfold institution had been actualized.

The call of Disciples from all quarters of the country took Mr. Campbell away from Bethany nearly half of his time. Kentucky and Ohio, Richmond, Washington, Baltimore, Philadelphia, and New York—away he went on the visits of his unofficial episcopacy over a reformation now numbering about 100,000 adherents. These absences placed additional burdens upon Robert Richardson, both in the editorial office and at the college. As usual, these were borne without fanfare—and without compensation.

At length he came to feel that a mockery of common justice was being perpetrated and finally protested to Campbell that he ought to be paid for these extra services. The president, in turn, said that the question was one to be settled by the Board of Trustees. In fact, he said, since a policy was needed to guide him in the future when like problems should arise, Richardson would be doing him a service to bring the matter before that body. This the doctor did in a special communication, dated July 3, 1843:

R. Richardson would respectfully represent to the Board of
Trustees of Bethany College that at the solicitation of the President of the Board, he consented to undertake in addition to the
duties of his own professorship, those of acting president of the
Institution during the necessary absence of Mr. Campbell upon
the business chiefly of the Board of Trustees.

In particular, the professor called attention to the fact
that during the preceding fall, for a period of seven con-
secutive weeks, he had served as acting president, dis-
charging his duties faithfully and to the best of his
ability. These duties, as he listed them, consisted "in
regulating classes—in attending upon morning exercises
and moral instruction—in admonishing the disorderly
both privately and publicly—in enforcing the discipline of
the Institution—in presiding at meetings of the Faculty—
in making the monthly reports—in corresponding with
persons abroad—and exercising a general supervision over
the affairs of the Institution at home."[11] He then reminded the trustees that it should be taken for granted,
"as a matter of course, as well as of right," that "compensation is due for services and responsibilities of this
nature, well known to be peculiarly onerous, and difficult
in the present instance."

He was compelled to refer the matter to the trustees,
he said, because the faculty, having a personal interest at
stake, was manifestly excluded from sitting in judgment
on the issue. The question was one which could be
legitimately decided only by the Board of Trustees, he
concluded. It was the trustees, he reminded them, who
had originally "fixed the apportionment of the Tuition
fees in general, but [they had] failed to make any regula-

tion to meet a case of this kind where one member of the Faculty is called upon to perform the duties of another in addition to his own."

The next day action was taken on Richardson's petition. It was a blunt reprimand: "On motion of John C. Campbell resolved That the duties of each Professor shall be to attend to all such classes and instructions as may be from time to time assigned to them by the President."

This decision of the Board of Trustees was received by the whole faculty with apprehension. It placed them under the personal dictatorship of one man; it gave them no means of redress when wronged; and, above all, it set a dangerous precedent for the history of the college. It was in a somewhat ruffled mood, therefore, that professors Richardson, Ross, Stewart, and Pendleton met to frame a protest, which they delivered to a special meeting of the trustees on March 19, 1844.

Saying that they knew that a new institution had many rough spots to be polished out and that a president should be allowed a great deal of freedom to lead, they nevertheless urged that when the freedom of the president to command was absolute, they were placed within the power of a dictator. They did not wish to suggest, they said, that the honored individual then occupying the office of president would take undue advantage of them, but in the future another man in the same position might make the lot of the faculty a miserable one. The principle was bad and if allowed to stand, it would soon set such a precedent that no professor in his right mind would engage to teach in Bethany College when he learned of it. The trustees, by their harsh and ill-advised resolution, had opened the door to abuses and contentions which the faculty now asked them to remove by rescinding their action. Their protest was long and vigorous. It was, in fact, a thinly veiled threat to resign in a group.

The matter was a "hot potato," and the trustees were inclined to avoid it as long as possible. No official action was taken that year. Meantime, President Campbell and the faculty were busy drafting their own solutions. The faculty proposed that it be authorized to assume the task of deciding its own division of responsibility democratically and that the president drop some of his teaching, which would then be reassigned. The president, on his part, prepared to recommend the appointment of another administrative officer, a vice-president.

President Campbell presented his detailed proposal July 3, 1845. Made wary by the spanking which the faculty had previously administered, the trustees withheld their action on Mr. Campbell's proposal until they could hear from the faculty. The faculty reported next day, accepting the following division of labor, slightly altered from the president's proposal:

Professor of Mathematics, with Mechanics, Hydrostatics and Pneumatics—Charles Stewart.

Professor of Ancient Languages with History—A. F. Ross.

Professor of Chemistry, French, Rhetoric with general grammar and Belles Lettres, Logic, Physiology and Botany—R. Richardson.

Professor of Natural Philosophy, Astronomy, Intellectual Philosophy, Political Economy, Geology and Zoology—W. K. Pendleton.

President—Sacred History, Moral Philosophy, Natural Religion and Evidences of Christianity—A. Campbell.

This report, too, was laid on the table until a special meeting of the Board of Trustees on August 13, 1845, when the proposal of the faculty was adopted, "subject to the alteration of the faculty." It was also at this meeting that the office of vice-president was created, W. K. Pendleton being named to fill it.

Robert Richardson had thus driven the trustees to recognize the faculty as a power in determining the policies of the institution and had also forced the adoption of a more stable administrative system. Ironically, he had acted both as bursar and as vice-president before either office was officially recognized or recompensed, and in each case the office and the pay had gone to another.

Dr. Richardson also assumed some of the duties of a dean of students. One proposal which he made to the faculty called for "a more careful supervision of the general deportment of the students, and a more intimate acquaintance with the actual condition of things in the institution, so as to be enabled to anticipate and prevent disorder." That this might be done, "sufficient time would need to be spent with the students, at their rooms, to form a personal acquaintance with them, and by inquiry and observation to learn their individual character, proficiency, habits, etc."

Having intercepted some students returning from Wheeling while he was making his medical calls, and having discovered that some members of the group were carrying liquor, he advised that "greater attention should be paid to prevent students from visiting neighboring towns without permission, and greater caution should be exercised in granting permission."

While thus engrossed in the college, Dr. Richardson was not idle as coeditor of the *Millennial Harbinger*. In a clever series entitled "Baptists Against Themselves," published in 1841 and 1842, he quoted a number of eminent Baptist divines as a means of putting to flight the more narrow-minded Baptists, who were rabidly attacking the Disciples. Fuller, Frey, Carson, and others yielded liberal quotations which fully supported the published sentiments of Alexander Campbell, so much so that "Discipulus" was able to exult: *"Out of your own mouths will I condemn you."*

He spoke a warning word against the excesses of a religion founded upon "revivalism" and dependent upon the continual excitement of big meetings: "Having been born amidst boisterous excitement, they can live in no other element. Receiving their religion from the inspiration of a preacher's voice, they are empty, cold, and joyless when he can be no longer heard." He advocated that these Christians, by the disciplines of teaching and searching, require themselves to go beyond conversion to Christian growth.[12]

He struck several blows against the rancor and intolerance of many contemporary Protestants. Mistaking doctrinal orthodoxy for the essence of Christianity, these carping critics were more devoted to "Partyism" than to Christianity. He even named names, flaying a certain Mr. Landis, whose attacks upon the senior editor were motivated from an "obvious design to widen rather than to close the broken ranks of the Protestant forces; to stir up strife, rather than to allay it; to judge and condemn with the sanctimoniousness of a Pharisee, rather than to examine and discuss" the questions at issue with candor and liberality befitting a Christian gentleman.

"The spirit of Christ is a spirit of universal benevolence and love," he continued in the same article, "and not one of the various parties of Christendom has been able, by all the barriers they have erected, to retain it exclusively within their own precincts. It was a want of confidence, a loss of Christian love, which first originated creeds. The different detachments of the Christian army would never have thought of thus fortifying themselves against each other, unless they had first begun to fear each other."

Nevertheless, not all intolerance and narrowness was to be found in the "sects." There were some gimlet-minded men in the reformation itself: "Others, too, who have even by profession chosen the broad ocean of divine revelation as their proper place, have, from . . . timidity, failed to carry out their declarations. They would rather beat about the estuary into which they were first launched, and keep carefully in view the well-known shores and land-marks." The truth of the matter is that "the Bible is too large and wide a basis for men of little minds."[13]

No topic of the day was more alive with misunderstandings than that of the Holy Spirit. It was commonly taught in Calvinistic circles that sinful man, wholly depraved as a result of Adam's "Fall," could not believe until a miraculous visitation of the Holy Spirit had bestowed upon him the "enabling grace." This visitation, in turn, was vouchsafed only to the "elect." Frontier evangelism, founded on such a premise, became an exceedingly emotional affair, consisting more in importuning God to be gracious than in calling men to repentance.

Against this view of the Holy Spirit, the Reformers resolutely set their face, as one man. They held that faith did not come as a result of the Spirit, but the Spirit came as a result of faith. To the mind of Richardson, some Disciples had reacted too violently against Calvinistic emotionalism and had adopted an opposite extreme of cold rationalism which denied any real place to the Spirit of God. These extremists, toward which position Campbell himself inclined, were called defendants of the "word alone" theory, and the adherents of the opposite view were known as the protagonists of the "Spirit alone" theory.

Coeditor Richardson launched into a discussion of these issues in a series of seven articles on "The Spirit of God," running through the years of 1842 and 1843, endeavoring to save the Disciples from a cold literalism, which he conceived to be as damaging as the florid Calvinism which it attacked. "These [emotional excesses in conversion] seemed to demand a remedy," wrote Richardson, "and, as after a feast the physician is apt to prescribe a fast, so it appeared to be then necessary to oppose this extreme by urging in the strongest terms the power and precedency of the word of God, and in the meanwhile to touch but slightly upon those operations called spiritual, which were considered as already carried to a dangerous extreme in the popular doctrines and practices of the day." In the same discussion, Richardson impaled one extreme literalist on the point of a joke:

An acute and ingenious advocate of the "Word alone" theory, a physician, and by a professional *extravasation* by no means unusual of late, a preacher also, was one day descanting upon spiritual influences to his congregation, and contrasting them with the power of divine truth. In the course of his sermon, he remarked "that many believed the Spirit to be distinct from the Word, and attempted to distinguish between them, and to show that there is really a spiritual agency or agent, other than the Word. This," added he contemptuously, "is a METAPHYSIC." Upon this incident, which actually occurred, I have to remark; that since, as a general division, we have but two chapters of human science—the one relating to matter and the other to spirit; or, as they are commonly termed, Physics and Metaphysics; and since the aforesaid Doctor evidently eschews the "Spirit alone" doctrine as a "*metaphysic*," it will logically follow, upon his own premises, that his own doctrine of the "Word alone," must belong to the other chapter, and be, consequently, a PHYSIC. If, then, even the Doctor's preaching be a *Physic*, its administration will not be, after all, so unprofessional.[14]

More mystical and devotional than any other man in the inner circle of the Reformers, Robert Richardson pleaded for a religion which left a large place for the Spirit, saying that evangelism itself was less important than a devotional mind:

> An immense number of proselytes may be made; multitudes may be added to the churches; periods of much animation and excitement may be enjoyed; but when we come to look for that for which alone all this preparation is made—an actual and spiritual union to Christ; spirituality of mind; devotion to God; creation anew in righteousness and true holiness—here it is that a lamentable disappointment occurs.

He wanted to leave no ambiguity, however: by the Holy Spirit he did not mean mere holiness of spirit. To be sure, the Holy Spirit does produce a disposition to holiness in the human mind, but it is inescapable that we are here dealing with "a real and literal something," not a spiritual state. "The Holy Spirit of God is imparted to the believer, really and truly, taking up his abode in his person, as a distinct guest, or inhabitant."

This literal indwelling of the Spirit of God in the Christian might seem disturbing to some, the doctor admitted, somewhat humorously, but, he admonished:

> Should any one say that he cannot understand how a human body can have within it, literally and truly, at the same time, two distinct spirits—the spirit of man, and the Spirit of God; I would reply, that . . . he may perhaps prove it to his own satisfaction *arithmetically*, if he will only *first* explain how ONE spirit can dwell in the human body, and then simply multiply his explanation by the figure *two*.

It is not so much *explanation* as *exercise* of the Holy Spirit that is needed, he said in another part of the series. "It is unfortunate that the abuses of the doctrine of the Spirit in popular theology, should have rendered many excellent and intelligent persons so extremely cautious upon the subject that, so far from cultivating religious feeling, they seem rather to repress it, and to seek to encase religion with the ices of a philosophical insensibility."

In fact, the doctor went so far as to say, if one must choose between one extreme or the other, between the "word alone" or the "Spirit alone" theories, it would be better to choose the latter for "there is one thing that can be said in favor of such views which cannot be said of the opposite theory, that they are at least *devotional*—that they *at least lead the mind to seek after fellowship with God; and embody the idea, so true in itself, and so con-*

soling to the Christian, that there is a real communion to be enjoyed with the spiritual world."

All of this, to Richardson's mind, should lead only in one direction: to an increased cultivation of the devotional life, something sadly lacking among Disciples. "The lesson may hence be learned, that, *just as man increases in religious light or knowledge, so should he increase also in warmth of feeling and fervor of devotion.*"

Richardson had been speaking of the "word alone" theory as "light without heat" because it was coldly intellectual; the "Spirit alone" theory he characterized as "heat without light" because it was almost exclusively emotional. What he wanted, plainly, was a combination of the two. Campbell, strongly influenced by the empirical philosophy of John Locke, was more than a little inclined to the *cold light* side of this comparison. In the course of this series, the senior editor had taken occasion, through a few footnotes, to snipe at his junior editor somewhat humorously by criticising his addiction to metaphors. "R. R." gave back as much as he received in this sally of wit, when he wrote, "But, being, it seems, 'addicted to metaphors,' I will add further, that if any man will show me his *light without heat*, I will engage to prove that it is nothing better than *moonshine.*"

Indeed, these articles on "The Spirit of God" in the *Millennial Harbinger* resulted from heated discussions between Richardson and Campbell. The latter was preparing for his forthcoming sixteen-day debate with Dr. N. L. Rice in Lexington, Kentucky, to begin November 15, 1843. For the purposes of this debate, Campbell had decided to defend the proposition that in conversion the

Spirit works "only through the word of truth." According to one contemporary of these men, Richardson sought to dissuade Mr. Campbell from championing so strictly limited a view. "He could believe what he chose, but he should not limit the Spirit publicly by the use of the word 'only.' Mr. Campbell could not see that to insert this word 'only' would be to deny in practice all he had taught in theory about liberty of opinion in things not scripturally established. But Dr. Richardson saw it."[15]

Many years later, writing to his friend Isaac Errett, Dr. Richardson commented upon Alexander Campbell's cold intellectualism:

> The philosophy of Locke with which Bro. Campbell's mind was deeply imbued in youth has insidiously mingled itself with almost all the great points in the reformation and has been all the while like an iceberg in the way—chilling the heart and benumbing the hands, and impeding all progress in the right direction.[16]

Richardson could foresee the shipwreck of the Disciples on this iceberg at some future time, as the faithful wrangled within a devotionless faith and a logic of mechanical literalism—unless the danger could be melted away by the sunlight of a new insight. He labored at that time and for many years following to liberate the Disciples from this benumbing literalism. He struggled to bring a spirit of tolerance and devotion into the reformation when it seemed to be trending toward a hairsplitting, fellowship-breaking logic, too little seasoned by Christian love. As long as Alexander Campbell was alive, that great mentor was able to hold these forces of reaction in check by the sheer weight of his personality; but after he was gone, Richardson felt sure, legalism would break all controls and do its perfect work of destruction.

As 1843 neared its close, Richardson observed that he had now written for two full series of the *Millennial Harbinger*, thus completing fourteen years of service. He acknowledged his authorship of all articles over his own signature or initials and also accepted the praise or blame for the articles signed by "any of the letters which compose the word L-u-k-e." It was his sincere hope, he said, that he had made a constructive contribution to the cause of the truth.[17]

In the next year he was to furnish a brief history of the Disciples for a volume on the story of religious denominations in the United States, to be edited and published by I. Daniel Rupp,[18] but not much else was written by him for the next three years. What he did not tell his readers in closing fourteen years of editorial communication was that his eyes had again deserted him and that he could no longer see well enough to read or write for the press.

When the doctor returned to Bethphage at the end of his arduous day of teaching and medical practice, he always put his horse in the stable, seeing that he was comfortable for the night, and then came on to the house, carrying the saddlebags with his books, apparatus, and medicines. He entered the house by the kitchen door. Once inside, the tired doctor hung his saddlebags on their peg, unwound the leggings which he always wore on horseback, and removed his boots with the bootjack. Slippered and housed, with wife and children about him, he was ready for the rest and the quiet of his home.

It was not the quiet of the recluse nor the silence of a man spent with fatigue, for an undying flame of purpose burned on in this man. Nearly fifteen years earlier he had given himself without reservation to the cause of religious reform, and no matter what labors he endured, he resolutely refused to give up.

He now ate supper and caught up on the news of the day at Bethphage. Rebekah, and the children: Nathaniel, Anne, Julia, Mary, David, and John—David had been born December 11, 1842, and John on July 23, 1845— all of them occupied his interest, and all who could talk were included in the conversation. In 1845, when John was a new-born baby, Nathaniel was past twelve, and the others ranged down the stairsteps of age in intervals of two or three years. Then there was the report from the hands on the work of the farm, and plans were made with them for the next day.

Often, when supper was over and all the reports had been heard and all plans made, the head of the house would take down a book from the family bookcase and read aloud. Likely as not, students would come over from the college, or other visitors—out-of-town guests or neighboring farmers—would drop in. He and Rebekah enjoyed company, and they encouraged people to come frequently, and in groups. These evening sessions ranged all the topics of interest, including religion, politics, agriculture. If farmers came in, it was the last, for the doctor was fast becoming an authority on scientific farming, to be consulted by all, far and near. In warm weather, this visiting took place on the large front porch, but in winter the center of hospitality was the large, homelike parlor.

Music was made one of the chief attractions of this home. When young people came, it was the chief diversion. There were two guitars, a flute, a piano, and a violin, in addition to a number of good voices. Even when the family was alone, they all gathered around the piano and sang hymns and popular songs. The doctor had a rich tenor voice and usually entered heartily into these domestic concerts. Sometimes he assisted with the accompaniment by playing the flute or violin. But before the evening had worn away many of its precious half-hours, the doctor had slipped away, out of the parlor through the kitchen and up the stairs to his study. There were assignments for tomorrow, articles to be written, books to be read, and thinking to be done.

How he made his preparation for classes toward the end of 1843 and through the months when "amaurosis" again assailed him, no one knows. These secrets he shut up with himself in the solitude of that book-lined room. With the music carrying up to him through the floors and through the candlelighted darkness, he did what was needful. Whatever the physical darkness, at least the flame of his purpose did not flicker or grow dim. The light by which he lived was not only clear; it was also warm.

Chapter X

DOCTOR ON HORSEBACK

RICHARDSON went everywhere on horseback. His spare, upright figure, astride his faithful horse, became an expected sight about the Bethany community. No matter what his errand—editorial, medical, or educational—he went to it and returned from it in the saddle. In the winter, his family rode in their fine sleigh, to the music of sleigh bells. In the summer, they used a coach or the spring wagon. But it was a rare thing for the doctor to set his foot inside either conveyance. Upon those occasions when he went abroad on a tour for the college or the *Harbinger*, it was with no little inconvenience that he undertook the journey, for on stagecoach and train, as in buggy or sleigh, he was miserably "seasick."

Saddlebags were always a part of his riding accessories. In one of the bags he carried his books, notes, and apparatus pertaining to his work in the classrooms of Bethany College. In the other he carried his herbs, leeches, drugs, and bleeding bowl to be ready for the work of a physician. While thus employed in transporting himself from one place to another all over Brooke County and sometimes beyond it as far as Kentucky, he was always thinking, planning, devising; and now and then he drew his horse to a stop to make a note in the worn leather notebook which he always carried. It was thus on horseback that much of the grist for classroom and printer, pulpit and Communion table were prepared, to be worked up into finished products in the study later.

As he rode to and fro between Bethany and Bethphage year after year, his horse seemed to grow almost a part of him. He had a great tenderness for this horse and a humane concern about other farm animals. One day the horse was lame. When he started out for college that day, his wife asked, "How are you going?" wondering if he would not have one of the hands drive him to town in the buggy. Intending to walk instead, he replied, "By Adam's express!"

Richardson's medical skill was dispensed without regard to compensation. The poor as well as the careless received help; frequently he gave them attention and medicine for which they never made an effort to pay. There are a large number of entries in the ledger that are charged, with the credit side of the page a complete blank. Many visits were made and medicine dispensed without pay; although each call was recorded in the ledger, no charge was entered. In such cases, the debt was forgiven at the time it was contracted. Some accounts were entered only to be marked "forgiven" at a later date.

Medical calls summoned him as far away as Wellsburg and West Liberty, four miles toward Wheeling, and to many remote corners of the county. Jane Campbell McKeever, Alexander Campbell's daughter, who was principal of Pleasant Hill Seminary for girls at West Middletown, ten miles distant, often sent her buggy for him, and the nauseated doctor, lurching over the road in this disturbing wheeled vehicle, made himself ill to attend to the sickness of a patient! Students and faculty members made frequent demands upon him in his capacity as a physician, and some of them even wrote to him after they had left Bethany, describing their symptoms and asking for his prescription by mail!

Hygiene and sanitation received his unflagging attention, both in the classroom and in his private practice. When called into a home by the illness of a member of a family, he inquired into the drainage about the premises, their habits of eating and sleeping, the care given their teeth, and the guarding of other normal bodily functions. At the college he emphasized these same things again and again. He felt that a physician should prevent disease as well as cure it. He saw to it that his own premises were kept clean and neat. Good living depended to no small degree, he felt, on a good physical environment and upon a proper care of the body. He never failed to emphasize safe food, good air, ample sleep, and helpful exercise; and he not only taught but practiced these things.

Dr. Richardson was very careful about carrying contagion. Once Rebekah greatly embarrassed him by a careless act of kindness which violated this rule. She lent a shawl to neighbors to protect a child that was being carried home during a storm, having forgotten that her own children had the measles. The result was that within a few days the neighbor's children all came down with the disease. It was a deeply chagrined physician who attended the sick in that case.

The families of Alexander Campbell, W. K. Pendleton, C. L. Loos, A. F. Ross, Robert Milligan, and others relied upon him as their physician. In caring for the family of Mr. Campbell, he was also frequently asked to treat one or another of the many prominent visitors and relatives who were always to be found at the mansion. In addition, the employees about the farms depended upon him. Sometimes during a severe illness where the condition was critical, he assumed the duties of both doctor and nurse, staying at the bedside throughout several successive nights and days, supervising diet and care, until his patient had passed the crisis.

As though all of this were not enough, the doctor sometimes rode away in the evening to attend a school meeting. He was interested in the public schools, then emerging on a national scale, and was a constant advocate of good school buildings and of educated teachers.

He also rode far and wide as a servant of the churches, preaching and teaching, and sometimes mediating church disputes. Once when a quarrel had broken out among the elders at Wellsburg, the church sent for the well-known peacemaker of Bethphage. A certain elder by the name of Berry was the cause of the quarrel. Having been successful in restoring peace, the doctor was telling about it the next day at his own family table. He remarked that he had learned in medical college that the juice of the elderberry was often good for fits, but in this case Elder Berry seemed to have caused the fit.

Richardson did not allow these constant calls of duty away from home to dull his keen delight in his own family. Conversation at table was spirited and happy. Family devotions made up a part of the pattern of each day. The parlor or front porch at evening, with visitors coming in more often than any Richardson went out, contributed vitally to a sense of family solidarity.

They all attended church together. The old Bethany church, built of stone, had been erected on the banks of the Buffalo in 1829, just inside the village. In 1852 it gave place to a larger building, made of brick. In both these buildings it was customary for the men to sit on the right-hand side and the women on the left. Two doors were provided, so that the sexes might enter the building separately. The narrow vestibule extending across the front of the church was also divided, so that the men might hang their coats on the racks, and the women might remove and hang up their riding skirts, before they walked in past the pulpit to take their places in the congregation, facing the doors. The Richardson children all sat with their mother, on the women's side. Since the light on that side was kinder toward his aching eyes, the doctor violated the general rule by sitting with them. When it came time for the singing of a hymn, his clear tenor voice was heard, soaring above the rest, and none of the Richardson throats were silent.

Robert and Rebekah's fourth daughter, the seventh child, was born on September 6, 1849, at the end of the first decade in the history of Bethany College. Her name was Frances, but from the beginning she was nicknamed "Fannie." As she grew she came to have a regal air about her which made her the acknowledged "queen" among the children.

Chemistry, French, logic, rhetoric, with general grammar and belles-letters, physiology and botany are the courses listed in the 1845-46 Bethany College catalogue to be taught by Professor Richardson. Except that he dropped French in 1849, this curriculum varied little throughout the next five years.

November 10, 1846, a brilliant graduate of the college and a student of languages, both ancient and modern, was added to the faculty. He was also employed as principal of the Family Institution at Point Breeze. It was the presence of Professor Charles Louis Loos, a brilliant linguist, that accounted for the shift in Dr. Richardson's teaching load at the end of the decade.

Salaries remained an "unfixed quantity" up until 1847, depending upon the share of the tuition divided out to each professor after the bursar's deductions, the janitor's wages, and the secretary's stipend were subtracted. In 1847, when ninety students were enrolled, an effort was made to peg the salaries at $800. They had often fallen below that. The continuously low level of his income made it impossible for Richardson to meet his mortgage payments to Alexander Campbell promptly, and it is a matter of wonder that he was able even as early as January 21, 1851, to deliver the last payment and receive Campbell's release.

An invariable feature of the college through all these years was the early morning chapel, held sometimes at 6:30 and sometimes at 8:00, with Alexander Campbell's or Dr. Richardson's lectures on the Bible. It was Campbell's custom to lecture almost the whole of the allotted hour and then close with a long prayer. Some of the young men occupying rear seats formed the habit of slipping quietly out of the room during these long prayers, to enjoy several minutes of unsupervised freedom before the beginning of the next class. Their absence was unnoticed because heads were bowed, Campbell was absorbed in his prayer, and the roll had already been taken at the beginning of the hour. The practice was still in its early stages, however, when Professor Richardson detected the defection and moved quietly to check it. One morning he had been detained in his classroom to care for some work of an executive nature and came late to chapel during the closing prayer. As he entered, he securely fastened the latch, turned the key in the lock, and dropped it into his pocket. He then took his seat at the rear of the hall. Presently he heard someone try the latch, fail, and return to his seat. Another did the same. Only when a third failed in his effort to open the door did it dawn on all the culprits that something had foiled their plans. The doctor was greatly amused. When the services ended, he applied the key and marched out at the head of the procession, without saying a word. Thereafter President Campbell's long prayers were attended unanimously.

To Robert Richardson, his work in Bethany College was no toilsome burden. It was a happy part of the great work to which he had given himself. He did it with enthusiasm. That enthusiasm is clearly reflected in his report on the 1848 commencement exercises:

We cannot withhold the opinion . . . that Bethany College is destined to rise still above its already high reputation; and, as it becomes better known, be also more and more appreciated for the combined excellences of its location, discipline, and instruction. No place could be more healthy or free from all demoralizing influences;—no discipline could be more parental and efficient; and the course of instruction, scientific, literary, moral, and reli-

gious, is without exception. We are assured it only needs a little
more time to enable Bethany College to take her stand among the
highest of our Literary Institutions, and to secure to her the widest
field of usefulness.[1]

About this time, Richardson became involved in the
emergence of another college. In 1849 and 1850, A. S.
Hayden, a convert of Walter Scott's, and Isaac Errett, a
self-educated liberal, were laboring on the Western Reserve to bring another college into being. Chartered in
1850 and located at Hiram, it was to be known during
its first seventeen years as Western Reserve Eclectic Institute, and then as Hiram College.[2] Both Errett and
Hayden consulted Richardson frequently while this new
institution was in its formative period. A letter from
Errett, then minister of the church in New Lisbon, Ohio,
the scene of Walter Scott's initial evangelistic success,
was dated November 12, 1849:

> We of Northern Ohio are at present intent on the establish-
> ment of a high school for boys and girls. [There had been some
> debate as to whether the institution should be of high school or
> college rank.] There have been held two conventions of Dele-
> gates, and the location of the institution is fixed at Hiram, Por-
> tage Co. The town of Hiram has subscribed $3,800. The inter-
> est on the subject is considerable in a number of churches. We
> think it probable that $10,000 may be raised for the erection of
> the school edifice, furniture, etc., etc. I am one of a committee
> of 3 appointed to draft a plan of government for the institu-
> tion—and also a charter to be presented to the Legislature this
> winter. We are to report to a Convention in Hiram next month.
> Knowing the interest you feel in the cause of education—and
> your experience in such matters, I write to request your advice
> and such suggestions as you may think valuable. . . . What ought
> to be embraced in the Charter? Will you be kind enough to

write soon and furnish as many thoughts as may occur to you in reference to the management of such an Institution? It will very greatly oblige me.

In the following letter, dated May 16, 1850, A. S. Hayden offered Richardson the presidency of the new school:

The ground is broken, and the foundations are actually laid. . . . The cost of the building complete, is estimated at about $10,000. Half of this is raised, and vigorous efforts are about being set on foot to obtain the rest. Our charter is obtained, a charter we think with provisions well suiting our purposes. A meeting of the Board of trustees was held this week on the ground and among other arrangements, a committee of two was appointed to negotiate for teachers; so if possible to have the school open at the completion of the building next fall. This is a delicate and responsible task imposed on Bro. Isaac Errett and myself; and we agreed, without any hesitation, first of all to consult with yourself on the subject. We scarcely allow ourselves to entertain the hope that it will be at all possible for you to disengage yourself from your very responsible and interesting relation to Bethany College. But we were unwilling to look in any other direction, until we first intimated our preference to you, and should receive a reply, and know whether there would be any reason or inducement for us to continue our correspondence with you on the subject. We feel that to no one within our acquaintance could we commit the charge of this institution, with a confidence quite so great as to yourself, in this, the most important period in its history.

Hayden solicited advice on all phases of the task in getting the new school under way: "We are all quite inexperienced in this kind of business, and any hints you may have time to offer in your reply will be thankfully considered."

Though flattered and intrigued by this request, and more than a little tantalized to try his hand at building up a new educational institution, Richardson decided that his love for Bethany and his duty there were too great to permit his acceptance. He did write fully and frequently to both men, however, taking a keen interest in the fortunes of the budding Eclectic Institute. Learning that A. S. Hayden himself had received the nomination to the presidency, Richardson wrote to Isaac Errett, a trustee of the new school, recommending Charles Louis Loos for the faculty. This former student of his had nearly starved as principal of the declining Family Institution, with an instructor's pittance for part-time teaching at the college added; and Richardson felt that a man of Loos's stature deserved a better fate. The letter from Bethphage is dated July 27, 1850:

I am happy to hear that Bro. Hayden has been induced to take the presidency of the school at Hiram. His connection with the institution I should think essential to its success. . . .

With regards to Bro. Loos he is at present just freed from his engagement with the Wellsburg brethren. He has been doing but little during the past year except practicing the lesson which it is so necessary for our preachers to learn; that is, how to live upon nothing. He has begun to fear that, like the horse of which the old Grecian tells us, he will die about the time he has attained to full proficiency in this mysterious art, and is desirous of securing a situation in which he can recruit a little. I have no doubt the situation you mention would suit him well if there be connected with it any reasonable and certain salary.

Bro. Loos is an excellent young man, very amiable, honorable and correct in his deportment. He is a fine scholar and is especially proficient in the languages. He is also well acquainted with the scriptures and with Bro. Campbell's course of Sacred History. . . .

There is one objection to Brother L.—his being a *German* and having of course the manners and the *mind* of a German.

Perhaps this one qualifying sentence prevented Loos from getting the post, for he went to a church at Somerset, Pennsylvania, instead. But it was not long until he was back in the academic world, where he fitted so admirably. He served a long period as a professor in Bethany College and was president of both Eureka and Transylvania Colleges. He was one of many of Richardson's students who became college presidents. If the doctor turned down this post for himself, perhaps he could supply others to hold it for him—many times over.

Beginning in 1847, the Richardson pen was again busy for the *Harbinger*. W. K. Pendleton was now added to the editorial staff, and he and Richardson were announced to the reading public as coeditors.[3]

Throughout the next three years, several important series of articles were to come from "R. R.'s" hand, articles which worked close to the center of Disciple concerns and which were to have widespread and enduring influence. He wrote nineteen pieces on "The Reformation," began his celebrated *Communings in the Sanctuary,* and wrote voluminously on education, religious education, popular reaction to excitement over the millennium, and even composed one piece upon child prodigies.

Since about 1830 the American scene had been alive with wild expectations of the Second Coming of Christ and the Last Judgment. Many of the Disciples, not excepting Walter Scott, were swept into the full tide of this excitement. Some even went so far as to set dates for the sublime event. To all of this speculation Coeditor Richardson turned a disapproving eye. Articles on the Second Advent then appearing in the religious press were like the tales of the Arabian Nights, he said: full of fancy and overstrained imagination. "But I greatly fear they have far exceeded the reasonable number of one thousand and one, to which the story-telling Arabians have been restricted, and that the effect of the whole has been to lead away the minds of men from the simple, yet great and precious promises of the divine word!"[4]

Nothing he did in this period was more vital than his articles on "Interpretation of the Scriptures." These appeared at frequent intervals over the next four years.

In this series Richardson started from the conviction that we have "no fallacy to fear in the Book of God, as we have in the books of men" and that "we are enabled to commit ourselves heart and mind to the word of God as to an infallible guide; an unerring teacher; and an ever faithful friend." As a consequence, we need have no fear about the soundness of the Bible as we read it; we need only to be on our guard against errors whose source is ourselves. "Our own perceptions may be at fault. We may fail to pay a proper degree of attention. Our minds may be biassed by preconceived opinions and theories. Our reasoning may be unsound, and our deductions false." As a scientist may take a false view of nature, so may a biblical student take a false view of the

Bible; and in both cases it is the method of study, not its object, that needs to be corrected. It was to such an aim of clarifying valid methods of biblical interpretation that the series addressed itself.

Interpretation of Scripture required intellectual and moral discipline, he said. Like any other field of inquiry, its meanings are open only to those who will study. A successful student of the Bible needs a teachable disposition, reverence for divine truth, prayer, as well as a knowledge of Bible history, Bible geography, and Bible chronology, manners, and customs. Also needed were an acquaintance with the history and religious views of ancient nations contemporary with the Jews, the grammar of the English language, the fundamental principles of rhetoric, and the laws which underlie logic and sound reasoning.[5]

He railed against the pompous ignorance of those who supposed that they could pick up the Bible and understand it without undergoing these preliminary disciplines:

They can speak with so much confidence, in unlicensed prose, of all the arrangements in the garden of Eden, that one would almost suppose them to have been there; and, as to the future, they feel themselves elevated upon the shoulders of both the lesser and the greater Prophets; and seeing, therefore, afar off, can tell you the very day, and give a shrewd guess as to the hour of the second Advent, and demonstrate the correctness of their views not only prophetically, but chronologically, arithmetically, hieroglyphically, pictorially, and almost geologically. To these persons there is nothing new or unlooked for, and . . . they wonder at nothing, unless it be at the only mystery which they admit to be inexplicable—to wit, that every body will not agree with them in their opinions.

Moreover, it was notorious that these same persons could not agree with each other!

Although he emphasized "the infallibility of the divine teachings," Richardson did not tie the inspiration of the Scriptures to the letter. "Ideas only, and not the words of scripture, were the dictation of the Spirit," he wrote. With regard to biblical authors he said, "They were not, then, properly inspired *writers*, but inspired *thinkers*; and delivered to us, each, in the language which he judged most appropriate, the thoughts suggested by the Heavenly Monitor."

Above all, our own preconceived notions and prejudices do us most harm when we are trying to understand the Bible. "It is against ourselves we must be upon our guard. We have to watch against our own imperfections in knowledge and capacity; our own prejudices and preconceptions; our own proneness to hasty and erroneous conclusions." It was with refreshing common sense that he observed: "However brilliant the light of heaven, it may not penetrate eyes that are closed."

The Scriptures possess no absolute and necessary power to make themselves understood. "Like the gold, the diamonds, and precious things of earth, the priceless gems of divine truth demand an earnest and diligent search, and can never be the reward of the careless and indifferent." The study of the Bible is as open as the study of nature and upon relatively similar conditions.

There is required, then, in the student of the scriptures, the same condition of mind necessary to the successful student of Nature. Both must have a just reverence for the common Author. . . . Both should have the same freedom from prejudice and prepossession, and both exercise the same care in observation. . . . The virulence and dogmatism of party spirit would be replaced by the calmness and liberality of the spirit of Christ in religion, . . . and we should have a happy end of strife and controversies.

Nothing is more germane to an understanding of the Bible than a recognition of the fact that it is a library containing a variety of literary forms. "The style of the Bible, however, is not uniform. It is not every where equally picturesque, metaphorical and ornate." Parables and allegories differ from one another, and each type of literature must be read in terms of its own meanings. A parable must not be interpreted as history, a law as an allegory, or a poem as prose.

Clearly, all that Richardson wrote on this subject was a part of the larger treatment of Christianity within a vital framework of devotion. At no time should the Christian aim at a learned dogmatism, but at "a *renovation—a regeneration* of the soul." Lacking this beauty of Christ within, Christians are "clouds without rain; trees that bear no fruit; failing fountains, which mock the thirsty traveler."

Chapter XI

DISCIPLE MANIFESTO

As the Richardson family moved into the 1850's it was in a nation boiling with activity of every sort. There were now 23,192,000 Americans. Ten million of these were living in the main basin of the Mississippi, and 120,000 of them were in California and Oregon. Driven by the potato famine, Irishmen had been pouring into America by the hundreds of thousands; in the previous ten years there were 1,700,000 immigrants. In this same decade five new states—Florida, Texas, Iowa, Wisconsin, and California—had added their stars to the national banner. The Gold Rush was on. Harriet Beecher Stowe was stirring up the hornets' nest of abolition. Only four years later Senator Sumner of Massachusetts, in the full heat of verbal strife over slavery, delivered his ardent speech on "The Crime Against Kansas" and was beaten into insensibility with a cane by Preston Brooks of South Carolina. In the year 1852 the Pennsylvania Railroad reached Pittsburgh, and the following year the Baltimore and Ohio made connection with Wheeling.

The Disciples were themselves an expanding frontier people, multiplying even more rapidly than the nation of which they were a part. In 1850 there were 118,000 of them; by 1860, there would be a quarter of a million. They were now organized in a huge cooperative body, having held their first national convention at Cincinnati in the fall of 1849, where they formed the American Christian Missionary Society and elected Alexander Campbell president of both the society and the convention.

For Professor Richardson the same steady pace of college duties continued. The faculty voted to impose a fine of five cents upon students for each class absence.[1] Pendleton and Richardson were appointed a committee "to have the tubes of the Fountain for the hall repaired so far as to conduct the water to Steward's Inn."[2] On March 9, 1853, the chemistry professor delivered a lecture on "The Atmosphere" to his class which so struck their fancy that they asked him to write it out to be published in their student journal, the *Stylus*. From the year 1852 the college session was shortened from ten to nine months, beginning October 1 and closing July 4.[3]

As in previous years, the doctor handled a large correspondence with former and prospective students. W. C. Rogers, a son of Elder Samuel Rogers, wrote from Elizaville, Kentucky, June 19, 1851, saying that he had been a student for three terms in Bacon College and that while he was then teaching school, he wanted to come to Bethany for his senior year, to prepare for the ministry. He mentioned the fact that he had worked his way while in Bacon College and continued: "My father Elder Samuel Rogers with whom you are acquainted is a poor man unable to assist me. Of course I contracted debts, while in Harrodsburg. After I shall have discharged these, my purse will be very light." Then he got down to the point. "Will you permit me to go one session and trust me a short time for remuneration?" he wanted to know. As an inducement, perhaps, he added: "Two young gentlemen I think will go from this Co. with me. They will pay their way in advance."

Two Hiram students—one of them to become president of the United States—were introduced to Richardson by a letter they carried, written by A. S. Hayden:

MY DEAR BRO. RICHARDSON,

The bearers of this are excellent young men, Bro. J. A. Garfield and Bro. H. B. Boynton, cousins, members of the Eclectic. We are happy in sending you a pretty full representation from Hiram this year; at least a dozen, came to enjoy the literary festivities of the fourth.

. . . .

Kindest love always to your family,

Yours truly,

A. S. HAYDEN

HIRAM

JUNE 25, 1853

A teacher at Maysville, Kentucky, who had graduated from Bethany College a short time before, wrote:

I am desirous of obtaining a situation where I can teach a small school and speak on Lord's Day. I have spoken frequently to some of the churches in this vicinity and can feel my strength increase at each effort. I have also been engaged in teaching but for several reasons do not like the location I had. . . . Remember me to all at Bethphage.

Your affectionate pupil

JOHN SHACKLEFORD.

Another graduate, J. S. Lamar, writing from Augusta, Georgia, on December 11, 1854, while in the midst of a difficult evangelistic effort, asked to be remembered to the family, stating that their "generous hospitality and courteous attention" had contributed greatly to his enjoyment of the years in Bethany.

In 1852 the Bethphage family grew by two more members. On September 2, twins were born! The startled parents named them Emma and Edgar. It was on December 20, 1856, that little Willie, the tenth and last child, came into the Richardson household.

Meantime the house at Bethphage had been growing to make room for all these children. As the family increased, Richardson kept adding rooms, until the original six-room structure now boasted nineteen, wings and annexes sprawling out in all directions. In this, Richardson was following the example of Campbell, whose fourteen children and many visitors had impelled him to a similar expansion at an earlier time.

A painful bereavement visited Richardson in this period. Nathaniel Richardson, his father, died September 29, 1851. Robert left his studies, his farm, and his patients to sit at the bedside of the dying man throughout the last week of his illness. The brief obituary notice, appearing in the Pittsburgh *Gazette*, gave no evidence of the poignant meanings which lay back of such a message:

DIED

This morning at 9 o'clock, N. Richardson, in the 73rd year of his age. The funeral will take place from his late residence, Allegheny, at 2 o'clock, this afternoon. The friends of the family are respectfully invited to attend.

Carriages will be waiting at the east end of the Old Allegheny Bridge, at 1 o'clock.

Long since, Robert and his father had been reconciled, and the two had found much joy in the flowering gardens about Bethphage, which the latter had planned and nursed along with loving care. He had also found much pleasure in his grandchildren. Now, the happy visits of Grandpa Richardson to Bethphage were over forever.

January 4, 1854, Thomas Campbell, father of Alexander—"Father" indeed to the whole reformation—passed to his saintly reward. He had often visited in the home at Bethphage and enjoyed the hospitality of the Richardson table. How amazed the children had been the first time they saw him take all his food, including dessert, onto his plate and mix it all together, remarking that it was all going to the same place and that the mixing might as well be done sooner as later! Doctor Richardson attended him as physician in his last illness and then assisted with the funeral. He wrote the obituary notice with a heavy sense of personal loss:

> I have to announce to the brethren and friends of the Reformation, the death of the venerable THOMAS CAMPBELL, Sr. He died on the evening of Wednesday, January 4th, having attained to the advanced age of ninety-one years, lacking about a month.
>
> . . . .
>
> Never was there an individual who manifested greater reverence for the Word of God, or a truer desire to see it faithfully obeyed. . . . And never was there one who more fully exemplified the doctrine which he taught, or whose life was more evidently guided by the teachings of the Spirit, and controlled by the Divine principle of love to God and man. . . . Oh, who that has enjoyed the pleasure of his society, can ever forget that countenance of benignity; those thoughtful eyes, beaming with affectionate regard; those venerable silvery locks . . . upon the high and ample forehead, and contrasting so agreeably with the

146

fresh and lively tints of his complexion; those kindly greetings and inquiries with which he so politely welcomed his friends; or that ready overflow of Christian feeling and instruction which he seemed unable long to repress within a heart filled with love and Divine truth![4]

While the Department of Agriculture was still an obscure bureau in the Department of the Interior, and before a weather bureau had come into existence, farmer Richardson was pioneering agricultural experiments and writing regularly to Washington, D.C., about crops, fertilizers, soils, and weather conditions. On December 28, 1855, he wrote to Dr. Daniel Breed, agricultural chemist of the Department of the Interior, one of a series of letters which passed back and forth between them. Discussing a technical question concerning fertilizer, Richardson stepped aside from the main issue long enough to admit, modestly, that his experiments at Bethphage had won him renown throughout Virginia:

> I live on a little farm and take great delight in agriculture. The Agricultural Society adjudged to me the ways for the best farming in this fertile portion of Virginia, but I must confess that I am by no means satisfied with my own methods. I am conscious indeed that they are very imperfect and that there is yet much to be learned as respects the proper application of scientific principles to agriculture.

He read up-to-date journals and books bearing on his hobby. The *American Farmer*, the *American Agriculturalist*, and the *Cultivator* came periodically to his study table. He filed the issues and had them bound for ready reference. Books like Johnston's *Lectures on Agricultural Chemistry* occupied a considerable section of his library.

But he was not content merely to read what others had written. He wrote up his own soil testings, crop rotations, and stock experiments, publishing them far and wide in newspapers and agricultural journals.

His neighbors, including Alexander Campbell, who farmed on a grand scale, respected and deferred to Richardson's leadership in the farming movement. Many of them gathered in the evenings at his house to question him and to hear the news of his latest experiments.

He was active at an early date in agitation and planning for agricultural colleges. W. L. Irwin, a Bethany College graduate living in Missouri, wrote him in 1853, for instance, asking him to outline a charter for an agricultural college in that state.

Later he published a detailed proposal for an agricultural department at Bethany, stating his hope that this would be America's first agricultural school.[5] His plans for the department, as disclosed in seven open letters to John C. Campbell, appearing in the Wheeling *Daily Intelligencer* for May 18 through June 27, 1855, outlined every phase of the subject from a full curriculum to buildings, classrooms, and laboratories. In the initial letter he praised J. C. Campbell for his prudent foresight some sixteen years before, which had secured the introduction of a clause in the Bethany College Charter "which gives to the Trustees of the Institution full authority to establish an Agricultural Department."

Richardson's "objects and arrangements of this Department" need not concern us here, but his final argument for educated farmers cannot be resisted: Maintaining that "farming is not the simple and ignorant occupation which many suppose," he declared that "the farmer has by virtue of his calling no inherent nor acquired right either to be a blockhead or to disfigure and impoverish, by his stupidity, any portion of the surface of God's earth, which may, indeed be his patrimony, but not the less that of the State and of mankind."[6]

Thus a professor of chemistry and a doctor of medicine, whose main interest was the reformation of religion and whose avocation was farming, antedated the proposal of the Merrill Act and, as a vigorous progressive, showed the way, far before his time, to a scientific agricultural economy.

The years 1853 through 1855 brought on another severe attack of eye trouble. Although the doctor wore glasses from his youth, this trouble was nothing that glasses could then reach. No treatment for it proved effective but rest of his vision. He bathed his eyes and face frequently in cold water to gain momentary relief from the pain, but the weakness continued, and deepened. This was his worst attack. When it did not lift, but dragged on, even increased, through three whole years, he began to fear that he would become blind.

Standing helplessly by as the doctor fought this battle alone was a fearsome experience for his family. His daughter Mary tells us about their apprehension and sorrow:

In order to endure more tolerably the hours of darkness that he felt approaching, he procured a flute and violin on which he practiced whenever he had a few minutes of leisure. This was generally in the evening between daylight and dark, and I seem to hear yet the plaintive strains of his favorite airs, such as "Life Let Us Cherish," "Oft in the Stilly Night," "Last Rose of Summer," etc., as they floated down from his study. Of course they were doubly sad and plaintive to us in view of the impending calamity.[7]

Amazingly, the afflicted doctor did not let his troubles halt his work. He continued his medical practice. His lecturing at the college went on without abatement. Pressing members of his family into service as secretaries, he even managed to get some reading and writing done—a great deal of it, in fact.

It was a matter of sorrow to him that he could not continue as coeditor of the *Harbinger*. That, plainly, was beyond the limits of his mortal strength. He chafed under his inability to contribute to the ongoing of the reformation in the way for which he felt he was best fitted, but his disappointment simply spurred him on in his search for other means by which he might serve the cause.

He went on tours. We find him meeting in a tent with Adamson Bentley, A. S. and William Hayden, Samuel Church, Isaac Errett, J. P. Robison, and W. K. Pendleton for a four-day rally called the "Annual Meeting at Bedford, Ohio."[8] D. C. Gordon reported having seen him in Baltimore in 1853.[9] He spoke several times at the "Re-Union at Allegheny City, Pa.," in November, 1854, and served on one of the committees.[10] On this trip he was helping with the college program to endow professorships.

In 1855 the trustees of Bethany College were laying plans for a campaign to get different states to endow chairs in the college. Dr. Richardson undertook to formulate and present the matter to Disciples in Ohio. A letter from Isaac Errett, dated April 20, 1855, reveals the progress being made at that time. "That Ohio will, with proper effort, endow a chair in Bethany College, is, I think, pretty well settled," he wrote. "That is the settled conviction and purpose of most of our leading brethren." But, as this same letter shows, Bethany College was now caught in the Euroclydon of the slavery strife:

> You are well aware that there is a very decided anti-slavery feeling in this portion of the State and that Mr. C's essays on slavery have given offense, and cooled the zeal of many in behalf of Bethany College. [Neither an abolitionist nor a proslavery advocate, Alexander Campbell took a position favoring the gradual, compensated liberation of slaves, as England had done.] There has been up this way a strong prejudice against Bethany from an impression that Southern students *ruled* everything there; and that Northern students had no equal chance. This however, is dying out. It has happened, unfortunately that most of our Northern students who had any brains, went South after graduating and your college has never been creditably represented in the North, save by Bro. Charles L. Loos.

The chief means, however, through which Richardson sought to perpetuate his efforts for the reformation was a little book published in 1853. It gathered together in brief form the contribution of the long series in the *Millennial Harbinger* on "The Reformation," running since 1847. He called his little book by a long name: *The Principles and Objects of the Religious Reformation, Urged by A. Campbell and Others, Briefly Stated and Explained*. It was printed on the presses in Bethany and published by Alexander Campbell. Mechanically it was a most attractive piece of work, and it was just 88 pages long. A model of brevity, comprehensiveness, and clarity, it was a work so fully expressive of all that the Reformers worked for that it deserves to be called the "Disciple Manifesto."

In announcing the publication of this book, Richardson himself said:

> As the feeble condition of my eyes renders it difficult for me to contribute much to the pages of the Harbinger, and has even induced me to withdraw my name, for the present, as co-editor in the work, I trust my friends and brethren will, by the circulation of this little work, enable me to hope that I am still thereby doing something in aid of the good cause in which we have a common, and, I trust, an abiding interest.[11]

Response to the book was enthusiastic. The circulation was extensive. Alexander Campbell's own reaction reflected the common mood:

> The author of this essay has himself been connected with it [the reformation] for almost a quarter of a century, and is well posted in its history from the beginning. This tract gives a well proportioned miniature view of it in a lucid and chaste style, and is worthy of himself and the cause. It ought to be circulated, not only among our brethren, but the religious and reflecting of all Protestant Christians. He is about having it stereotyped in Philadelphia, that it may be cheaply and extensively circulated through the country.[12]

A year later, Coeditor Pendleton could report to the readers of the *Harbinger* that the demand for the book was still strong: "We are gratified to learn that the brethren have shown their appreciation of this little work, by the liberal orders which they have sent in for it."[13] The book was to go through three editions and un-numbered printings, not only during the author's life, but for many years after his death.

Believing, as did other Protestants, in the authority of the Bible, but, contrary to most of them, in the equal right of all Christians to interpret the Scriptures for themselves, and without reference to theological dogmas, the author stated the program of the reformation as an effort "to establish a *unity of faith*, instead of that *diversity of opinion* which has distracted religious society; and to restore the gospel and its institutions, in all their original simplicity, to the world." Its dominant purpose, he said, was "*to establish* CHRISTIAN UNION *upon the basis of a* SIMPLE EVANGELICAL CHRISTIANITY."[14] The movement rested upon three principles: "1st. The distinction between FAITH and OPINION. 2d. The distinction between what may be emphatically termed THE CHRISTIAN FAITH and the doctrinal KNOWLEDGE. 3d. The true BASIS OF CHRISTIAN UNION."[15] From these basic principles stemmed six "objects," which were regarded as instrumental. These may be summarized as follows:

1. The discovery that the revelation recorded in the Bible is not level but progressive, disclosing itself through dispensations.

2. The discovery that the church began, not in Jewish times, but at Pentecost, and is therefore not to be confused with Old Testament institutions.

3. The action of baptism (immersion), and its design (remission of sins).

4. The place of the Holy Spirit.

5. Weekly Communion.

6. Autonomy of the local church.

Coming to the first principle, Richardson said that the whole effort of the Campbells and others was to uncover at the heart of a great mass of theological speculations, the solid core of "common Christianity." This, they held, is to be found in the empirical facts of Scripture. Christianity is primarily a deed, not a dogma; the deed must be kept central, but the rise of dogma is inevitable. This situation is to be resolved by adherence to the following proposition: "Each individual must have a perfect right to entertain what opinions he pleases, but he must not attempt to enforce them upon others, or make them a term of communion or religious fellowship."[16]

It is in his discussion of the second principle that Richardson rises to the heights. "The Christian Faith" is not to be confused with "knowledge" or intellectual belief. At this point, the Disciples differed from other religious bodies in "one important particular," namely, that these bodies supposed Christian faith was *doctrinal*, while the Disciples maintained that it was *personal*. "In other words, they suppose doctrines, or religious tenets, to be the subject-matter of this faith; we, on the contrary, conceive it to terminate on a *person*—THE LORD JESUS CHRIST HIMSELF."[17] "The Christian faith . . . is personal in its object, leading to personal regard and love for Christ, and a personal interest in his salvation." This faith does not consist in definitions; it is not concerned with the "litigated questions" upon which sectarianism feeds.[18]

It is important, says the author, to know what the Christian faith is *not*: "It is to be noted, that to believe in Christ is not simply to believe what Christ says; that is, to receive as true whatever may be regarded as the teaching or doctrine of Christ. . . . Again: to believe in Christ is not merely to believe that there lived a person bearing that name."[19] What, then, does it mean to believe in Christ? Richardson's answer is clear:

> To believe in Christ, is to receive him in all the glory of his character, personal and official; to trust in him in all the relations which he sustains to us; . . . to behold in him our only hope and refuge; and renouncing ourselves, our own self-confidence, our righteousness, and every vain device, to lean on him only as our stay, and to look to him only as the "Lord our Righteousness," as our salvation and our life. It is . . . to trust in him as *our* Saviour, to walk with him as *our* teacher, *our* friend; to realize his gracious presence with us, and to discern his foot steps in the path we tread. It is to be brought into *direct relation* and *fellowship* with him; to think of him as a *person* whom we know, and to whom we are known; to speak to him as to one who hears, and to listen to him as to one who speaks.[20]

Such a faith in Christ, declared Richardson, "is the CHRISTIAN'S CREED, and the only creed to which any one may be justly called upon to subscribe."[21]

As for the third principle, Christian union, it is not to be confused with mere *unity* or *uniformity*. Like the Christian faith, which is its only secure foundation, it is vital, dynamic.

As Christ is himself the chief cornerstone of the church and its only foundation, so also is he the true basis for the reunion of its splintered fragments. To substitute "an exact knowledge of remote points of Christian doctrine" as the basis of union would be "as unscriptural as it would be irrational to prohibit men from enjoying the light and warmth of the natural sun until they had first attained a high proficiency in astronomy."[22]

The reasonableness, the tolerance, and the catholicity of this book breathe their spirit through every paragraph. In them we discover no internal struggle toward faith, only calm serenity; no human bitterness, only love; no inclination to admit defeat by untoward circumstances, only resolute purpose.

When Isaac Errett came to Bethany in the spring of 1854 to deliver a course of lectures, not all eyes were upon him. With growing appreciation, many were beginning to single out side-bearded "Dr. Richardson, with his hacking little cough, and his varied and vast attainments," who was spoken of as "the saintly."[23]

Chapter XII

"COMMUNINGS IN THE SANCTUARY"

By 1856 the long deep valley of shadows in which Robert Richardson had been walking for the past three years yielded to a tableland of returning vision. He was able to go back to his post on the staff of the *Millennial Harbinger*.[1]

Robert Milligan, professor of mathematics in Bethany College, was also added to the staff. Before coming to Bethany in 1855, Milligan was a member of the faculty of Indiana University, at Bloomington, and had previously taught in Washington College, his alma mater, in Washington, Pennsylvania. A rising young star of the reformation, he was a brilliant teacher and a writer of great promise. The senior editor heralded his coming and the reappointment of the other editors in the following words:

> We are happy in informing our readers that we have secured to our Editorship, as Associate Editors, Professors Richardson, Pendleton, and Milligan, who will henceforth furnish contributions to our monthly bill of fare. The additional expense incurred by this arrangement, will be a new argument with those who appreciate our conjoint efforts to make the Harbinger still more worthy of the cause we plead, and still more interesting to our readers.[2]

One reason why Alexander Campbell needed so many associate editors was that his own iron-bound constitution was beginning to weaken. His sixty-eight years had been hard-driven ones; to a man of lesser endurance, they would have been health shattering long before. The flame of his mind, which had previously shone so brilliantly and so steadily, now flickered. There were times of sustained radiance of the old sort, but these faded again into the dimness which claimed him more often and for longer periods.

This doleful news about the Patriarch of Bethany was not the sort of thing that any Disciple would commit to print, but it was known and sorrowfully discussed in the inner circle, and in the wider circles many guessed it. This circumstance makes the waning of Mr. Campbell's powers a thing exceedingly hard to document, but the certainty of it is so clear to those who now know most about him and his family that it seems impossible to doubt it. Besides, there is a letter written by W. K. Pendleton to his daughter "Cammie" on June 2, 1854:

> Your grandpa has not been so well lately as he generally is. He complains a good deal of debility and seems almost overcome with the weight of his labors. He is from home now spending some days at a water cure established in Ohio river near Pittsburgh.[3]

Associate Editor Richardson got right into the swing of his work with a series on the "Nature of Christian Faith." In its main features, this series was really a re-affirmation of his pronouncements on "The Christian Faith" in his book, *The Principles and Objects of the Religious Reformation.* "Protestantism," he asserted, "is, in its very nature, a grand *doctrinal controversy.* It has never been a converting power for Christ."[4]

The strife among the denominations was rooted in an equating of *faith* with *knowledge,* that is to say, the supposition that the Christian life and Christian belief are identical. "Hence conversion has come to be not so much a change of heart as a change of head."

Richardson pleaded for something very different, for a Christian doctrine which would be truly spiritual and vitally unifying: "Let not an intellectual assent to points of doctrine be mistaken for the Christian faith. But let this faith be allowed to stand forth in its true character, as a *personal trust* in Christ, and let the doctrines of Christianity be the study of those who are already converted to Christ." "The primitive Christian faith, as defined by Paul, is simply 'trust in Christ.' . . . Christ is not a doctrine, but a person. . . . Faith is just as personal as love or hope, and the same perversion which makes faith doctrinal, makes love also doctrinal, and hope a theory. It is not the love of Christ that animates the sectary, but love of the system. . . . It is not Christ that is formed in him 'the hope of glory'; but an intolerant spirit of bigotry and spiritual pride."

For this there was a cure. "It is the characteristic feature of the present reformation to endeavor to disentangle the Christian faith from doctrinal controversy." What was required was not a new organizational alignment, but a change of spirit. This could begin within any church or denomination; indeed, it had already begun in many places. Individuals are found everywhere "who, though *in* sects, are not *of* them," men and women "who constitute, indeed, the only true people of God on earth."

In a series on "The Misinterpretation of Scripture," a sort of sequel to the series on "Interpretation of the Scriptures," Richardson revived the discussions which he had prolonged over several years prior to his latest attack of "amaurosis." He also, the following year, 1857, had occasion to direct several well-aimed blows at "spiritualism," which was then agitating the religious public.

He took time, as well, to give his hearty approbation to the "Revision Movement" then afoot to produce a new version of the Bible.[5] In the translation of Scripture out of the original Hebrew and Greek languages, he himself was something more than an amateur. His *Harbinger* articles dealing with Bible texts reveal a careful study of them and a thorough acquaintance with translation problems. In his own sermons, meditations, and discussions he used the Scriptures with deference for the accurate and precise meanings of their original. Faulty translations received his critical attention. A case of particular interest is that of his calling attention to the inaccurate rendering of the last clause of 2 Timothy 2:15; thirty years later, the translation he suggested as correctly conveying the meaning of the original was the one adopted by the American Revision Committee. It is therefore not surprising that he not only belonged to the American Bible Union, paying the high fee for life membership, nor that he contributed out of his scholarship many specific suggestions for the revision itself. A letter from New York, March 20, 1854, confirms this:[6]

"COMMUNINGS IN THE SANCTUARY"

My Dear Brother,

We thank you for the remittance and the criticism. To me the force of the criticism appears irrefragable. I will pass it over to the revisers, who will give it due attention.

Very affectionately,

WM. H. WYCKOFF

The verse, "Except ye eat the flesh of the Son of Man, and drink his blood, ye have no life in yourselves!" (John 6:53), was discussed in a footnote with this comment:

This passage is incorrectly rendered in the common version, "Ye have no life in you." The true sense is thus quite lost. For, to say that any one "has life *in him*," is a very different proposition from this: that "he has life *in himself*." The former denotes merely the possession of life; the latter implies not only this, but that the life possessed is an essential part of the nature of the person of whom it is affirmed.[7]

With all the children born and growing, and with visitors coming in larger numbers, Bethphage became increasingly dear to Richardson. Now, however, he came with some shock to the time when his fledglings began to leave the nest with their own mates. Anne was the first of these. On July 8, 1856, she was married to J. M. Dunning of Missouri and departed for the West.

Nearly twenty years of possession had transformed his home and farm into the image of the doctor's own personality. Studying London's *Encyclopedia of Trees and Shrubs*, he grew every kind of fruit indigenous to the climate of Virginia's northern panhandle. He did his own grafting of plums, cherries, and apples. Spraying his trees frequently and looking over them carefully, he assured himself that insects were not spoiling the fine quality of fruit in which he prided himself. He also planted his own wheat, sowing it by the method as old as the world, scattering it with his hands. The hired help about the farm were trusted to do most of the work on his orders, but the sowing of the yearly wheat was a ritual that he reserved strictly for himself.

It was a great day in the fall at the Richardson home when the time came to make apple butter. Juice was pressed from some of the apples and made into cider. Other apples were pared and cored for the making of apple butter, which was cooked in large kettles over open fires in the yard.

Not long after apple butter time came butchering. Here again, Richardson supervised. He himself always shot the animal to be butchered, being, queerly enough, a very good marksman. Hams and sides and shoulders were hung in the smokehouse for the process of curing in the smoke of a hickory fire that had to be built just right and kept burning for just the proper length of time.

A flail was used for threshing, and a fan mill in the barn cleaned the grain. No farm machinery was allowed to stand in the field encountering the weather but was carefully stored in the barns and sheds. Tools were kept in repair and sharpened, as the following item from the doctor's diary demonstrates: "A saw should be set before sharpening; it may be set by a nail on the end of a log. For sawing across the grain should be filed as slanting as possible, to give each tooth a sharp edge. For ripping should be filed straight across nearly."

The farmer of Bethphage was greatly interested in Irish potatoes and was even instrumental in introducing the Early Rose and the Blue Meshanio varieties of this vegetable to his part of the country. Then as now insect pests bedeviled the gardner, and the Richardson children were pressed into service to "pick potato bugs" off the patch near the house.

Mrs. Fannie Thompson, a daughter, told of a morning following a day of picking potato bugs when her brothers and sisters awoke to find their hands and faces a mass of blisters. Chemist Richardson went into immediate action and analyzed the secretions of some of the bugs. He discovered that they were about the same as those of the Spanish fly, which was then used by physicians for "blistering." Thereafter, the children never again picked bugs with their bare hands.

Emma, one of the twins, disclosed one of her father's weaknesses—for public auctions! "He would ride away to a public sale, spend half a day talking with the farmers, and come home bringing articles he had bid up to help the sale along, that we very often could make no use of, to my mother's great amusement."

The Richardson children attended school in Bethany; their teacher for many years was Miss Jane Smith, who taught all the children of the Bethany community in a little school building not far from Bethany's old stone church.

Through four years of the *Millennial Harbinger*, from 1847 to 1850, Coeditor Richardson published over his own name a continuing series of devotional essays under the title "Communings in the Sanctuary." These were really Communion talks which he had delivered in the Bethany church. Later on, twenty-four of the best of these meditations were gathered together to make the Disciples' first and most celebrated book of devotions. It was published by the Transylvania Press, but unfortunately the year is not known.

J. W. McGarvey recalled these talks in his student days while attending services in the old Bethany church. "The richest service of all," he said, "was when they had a sermon by Mr. Campbell followed by Dr. Richardson in a five or ten minute talk at the Lord's Table."[8] He said that these talks were gems of beauty.

Other students set the scene for us and enable us to enter into the atmosphere of reverence which the doctor created by these talks. Never did high priest enter the holy of holies with a more genuine reverence than did Dr. Richardson enter upon his duty on these occasions. By his timid and reserved manner he seemed to apologize for his presence at the Communion table. His words came slowly and even timidly, at first, and a stranger would have been ready to sympathize with him because of his apparent embarrassment; but after a sentence or two, one forgot the timidity in listening to the tender, pathetic, and quietly eloquent words which fell from his lips. His words in these meditations were in the form of prose, but they were the essence of poetry. Possibly Richardson was the only man among the polemical and didactic Reformers who spoke and wrote devotionally.

The public worship of God was to him an art requiring not only the finest preparation of the service but the

erection, as well, of church buildings expressive of a wor-
shipful purpose.

Though we may indeed dispense with the "long-drawn aisle
and fretted vault," the clustered pillars, the gorgeous tapestry,
the carving and the gilding which merely gratify a love of
worldly splendor, surely a decent respect for the service of the
house of God should induce a careful attention to every means
calculated to favor devotional feeling, and sanctify those rites
whose mysterious import claims the undivided attention of the
soul!

How often may we justly impute to the absence of such aids,
that want of reverence which is so conspicuous! How often are
those wandering thoughts, those restless glances, those distracted
feelings which are so readily marked, occasioned by those un-
propitious arrangements by which the things and thoughts of the
world are continually pressed upon the attention![9]

A lively sense of the presence of God seemed to the
doctor to be the very soul of religion. Man has immense capacities:

Placed, as it were, in the middle position of the universe, and
blending in himself the material and the spiritual, he can reach
to the lowest ranks of being, and also to the highest—even to
God himself. He can contemplate every phasis of life and
every variety of nature. Collecting the traces of the divine
presence in his works, he can connect them with the Being from
whom they issue, and, ascending upon the wings of Faith, hold
sweet communion with the Infinite and Eternal One.

To establish and maintain this communion is the great end of
religion. To unite the soul to God; to erect in the human heart
a living temple for his abode; to secure the enjoyment of that
divine presence which is the earnest of eternal blessedness: these
are its noble and exalted aims—its truest, holiest purposes.[10]

To him there was nothing impersonal or mechanical about the relation between man and God. No legalistic system of salvation would answer to his demands:

> But Christianity is very far from being a mere system of redemption from sin, or salvation from punishment, or selfish rewards for obedience. It designs not only to bestow remission of sins, but to effect a *renovation*—a *regeneration* of the soul. Indeed, it is not too much to affirm that *it can be a means of salvation only as it is a means of renovation*. . . . "In Christ Jesus," nothing is of the least avail but "a new creature."[11]

Having met his own hours of dark despair, the doctor could write with authority when he said: "It is especially amidst the abodes of sorrow, and in the dark hours of affliction, that we are likely to be found nearest to the 'man of sorrows and acquainted with grief.' . . . It is amid the disappointments of life; in the days of mourning and of desolation; in the hours of self-abasement and penitential love, that we meet with Jesus."[12]

> The sanctuary of God is the house of Memory and of Hope. . . . It is here that the two sacred institutions [baptism and Communion], which unite to commemorate the death and the resurrection of Jesus, harmoniously blend also the extremes of human destiny, and, reconciling grief with joy, unite the darkness of the grave with the light of life.[13]

In these essays are many surprising and delightful epigrams and gleaming insights: "How little we know of life, although it is every-where around us, and even within us!"[14] "Alas! how vain are tears of grief, or words of penitence, or promises of amendment, when the grave has hidden from our eyes the neglected or the injured!"[15]

"It is not mere formal adoration of a carved, a graven, or a molten image that constitutes idolatry. On the contrary, it is the giving the heart's affections to anything that is not God."[16]

It is only in the atmosphere of prayer that Christian growth can take place. Robert Richardson believed that devotional disciplines were indispensable to progress in the religious life:

> It is the contemplation of infinite excellence that exalts, as it is the society of the good and the noble that inspires nobility of soul. Unable of ourselves, perhaps, to form high conceptions, and, without "the bold warmth that generously dares," we catch, by degrees, something of the soaring spirit of the virtue that belongs to the noble minds with which we enjoy habitual intercourse, and thus learn to share and to imitate the excellencies we admire. It is thus that communion with Perfect Goodness shall lead us to be good. Infinite Holiness and Purity shall inspire us with pure and holy affections, and the love of God, awakening in the heart a kindred emotion, shall transform the soul and invest our nature with a divine beauty.[17]

Chapter XIII

"SLINGS AND ARROWS"

THE YEAR 1857 Robert Richardson spent under bombardment. "The slings and arrows of outrageous fortune" were aimed at him from many directions. A part of these adversities were "acts of God," but most of them were, in their origin, "human, all too human."

In the college, at the beginning of the year, florid dreams of the future were mushrooming. With student enrollment higher than ever and public favor mounting, the faculty and administration were beginning to see visions of an ambitious program of expansion. Within the United States there were now 122 colleges with a total of some twelve thousand students. In addition, there were forty medical schools, forty-four theological seminaries, and sixteen law schools.[1] Although the nation was riding headlong toward civil conflict, it was always possible to believe that war could not come, to plan as though it would not.

J. P. Robison and Isaac Errett, trustees of Bethany College, were pushing the creation of a distinct "theological department" and to that end were seeking the repeal of the section of the charter prohibiting theological instruction. They entertained hopes that this department would become a separate school with its own buildings. In this they were blocked by the state legislature, but expectations in other areas of the college continued undaunted.[2]

In March, 1857, Associate Editor Richardson began a series of articles on "Faith *versus* Philosophy," which ran throughout the year.[3] The series was based on the text, "Beware, lest any man spoil you, through philosophy and vain deceit, after the tradition of men, after the rudiments of the world, and not after Christ" (Col. 2:6). Before they were finished, these articles were to involve him in spirited controversy with President Tolbert Fanning of Franklin College in Tennessee. This controversy, in turn, was to provoke attacks and misrepresentations which would come to the ears of Alexander Campbell and drive a wedge of misunderstanding between him and Richardson.[4]

Richardson undertook the series from no contentious motives, but, rather, from the conviction that a large and dangerous minority within the reformation were being led by men of little minds and imagination to substitute a theory of faith for faith itself. It was a gallant stand against the intolerant bibliocentric literalism from which Campbell was trying to save Protestantism. It was a courageous effort to advance the cause of a spirituality that was centered in devotional loyalty to Christ.

Although the membership of the Disciples was now approaching a quarter of a million and was supposed by its adherents to be twice that large, Editor Richardson asserted that it had as yet by no means accomplished its design "to restore pure, primitive, apostolic Christianity, in letter and spirit, in principle and in practice." Some, he said, numbering himself with them, "are apprehensive that there has been an exchange of opinions, rather than a change of condition; a readiness to propagate and defend a theory, instead of a willingness to make progress toward that perfection which the gospel enjoins."

Clearly there was something wrong somewhere in the reformation. Where could the trouble lie? There were three possibilities: it might be (1) in the basic principles of the movement, or (2) in the practical program for implementing the principles, or (3) "it is possible that some system of human philosophy has insidiously intruded itself, and, like the serpent in Eden, seduced the unwary, by the charms of forbidden knowledge." Examining, in turn, the first and second possibilities, he concluded that they must be rejected.

Certainly, Richardson said, the Disciples have no lack of proselyting power. In fact, an inordinate zeal for getting members has become too often a "heartless and superficial formalism." A wiser view of evangelism would hold that Christianity is designed, not merely to bring together a multitude of adherents, but to save the world. "Its design is to make *converts* and not *proselytes*." Feverish efforts to herd large numbers into the churches, with no apparent thought for the future, is both shortsighted and self-defeating. "It is not the planting that can be made a substitute for the fruitage; nor the sowing for the harvest."

With regard to church organization, Richardson wanted it clearly understood that he did not "undervalue the importance of a scriptural order." On the other hand, "It is not organization that can impart life." Reliance on "mere *forms* and *names* or *titles*" that had been emptied of their original New Testament content had made of many a church officer "a sort of spiritual *undertaker*, [rather] than . . . a physician of souls."

The cause of the malady in the brotherhood was, in short, neither lack of evangelistic zeal nor want of concern over organization. It was the introduction of privately held philosophies as public tests of faith. Having professed to abandon "speculations," many Disciples had only supposed themselves to have done so. In reality they were entertaining philosophical assumptions unawares, and these assumptions were adulterating or displacing the faith. Because of such assumptions, "the efforts of some of the most able advocates of the cause have been misunderstood and perverted."

Tolbert Fanning, president of Franklin College and editor of the *Gospel Advocate*, had previously criticized Richardson, so the doctor now returned the compliment by observing that Fanning was himself an ideal illustration of what he was talking about. Though denouncing all philosophy as leading to infidelity, Fanning was himself a dogmatic follower of John Locke. There is nothing wrong with this, said Richardson, until one lifts such dogmas out of the realm of private opinion and seeks to impose them upon others as Christianity itself.

Exactly what is it that Fanning believes and is confusing with Christianity itself?

> According to this philosophy of man, he can receive no impressions except those from material things around him, so far as either his mental or bodily constitution is concerned, and he is consequently by nature a materialist, utterly incapable of deriving either from the external world or from his own soul, any conceptions of spirit or spiritual things. For these he is wholly

dependent upon revelation, that is, upon words, divine communications addressed to the bodily senses, which are, in this system, regarded as the only avenues to the soul.

To substitute such a "dirt philosophy" for a warmly personal Christian experience was a tragedy. It tends to "unfit men's minds to receive anything that is not merely outward and formal" and "gradually dries up the fountains of spiritual sympathy."

According to this philosophy, the operation of the Spirit is limited to the word alone, a view which issues in "a blind, unreasoning partiality, which, in reality, degrades the Bible, by placing it in a false position, and ascribing to it exclusive power and attributes which it never claims for itself."

Locke is right, agreed Richardson, in placing "facts first, then testimony, then faith, then feeling, then action." But when facts and testimony are exaggerated all out of proportion to the rest of the series and faith is reduced to a mere "belief of the historic facts presented in the gospel," this is a sad defection, for "true Christian faith reaches *beyond* the recorded facts to the PERSON concerning whom the facts are related. It is CHRIST himself, and not any, nor all of the facts in his history, that is the true and proper object of this faith."

In a reply characterized by fallacious reasoning, Fanning floundered to a number of erroneous conclusions. Since Richardson had attacked the "word alone" theory of conversion, Fanning supposed that he flew to the opposite of "spiritualism." Although holding unconsciously to the Lockian philosophy as being the true interpretation of the universe and man and thus the only valid approach to an understanding of Christianity, Fanning bitterly denounced the teaching of natural theology in colleges as rank "infidelity." When he learned that Alexander Campbell himself had for years taught exactly such a course, he declared that if such were the case, Campbell had abandoned his earlier position. "We cannot, and will not believe it." It was not far from this to a denunciation of the professors of Bethany College for teaching infidelity.

For his part, Richardson was as much opposed to unrestricted mysticism or "spiritualism" as he was to the "dirt philosophy" of Locke. The whole point of his series was that no philosophy should be substituted for Christian faith; no intellectual system should be allowed to take the place of an inner quality of life. "A profession of Christianity which does not produce a marked change in life, a transformation by the renewing of the mind, and an entire consecration to God; . . . which, on the contrary, leaves those who make it, conformed to the world in its fashions and its follies, occupied with worldly speculations and selfish interests, full of arrogance and ambition —is manifestly far from being a genuine profession of the gospel."

Referring to Fanning only to "exhibit him as a full-bodied specimen" of a Lockian dogmatist, as he explained in a letter to Philip S. Fall, Richardson did not plan to engage in a discussion with him. But Campbell thought it necessary to publish Fanning's reply, "lest he should have ground to complain of unfairness." The reply was given space in the *Harbinger*. It inflamed the controversy and spread it widely over the brotherhood.

What disturbed Richardson even more than this, however, was, as he told Mr. Fall, that "Brother C— greatly disapproved of my article and even told me that if a portion had not been printed before he saw it he would not have suffered it to go into the Harbinger." How could he account for such an attitude, in view of the fact that the position taken in the "Faith *versus* Philosophy" series was exactly that which Campbell had himself set forth so admirably in *The Christian System* in 1836! He could assign only one cause, a cause for which he had other evidence as well: "Some one, I think, has been poisoning his mind latterly with the suspicion that my articles were really directed against his teaching. Yet I do not know how I could have used greater care or delicacy in avoiding even a seeming conflict."

Campbell's rebuke did not, however, reduce Richardson's esteem for him:

> Of course, I shall pay no regard to this little ebullition of jealous feeling. Brother C. is getting old. He has been a faithful laborer and perseveres still even when his work is done— may peace ever attend him! Still each one has his own duty to perform, and he ought not to stop others from doing their portion of the work, or put viewpoints into the hands of such a man as Fanning, against his true friend, and, what is still more unfortunate, against the cause of truth and Christian progress.

Unfortunately, the debate kindled by the publication of Fanning's reply in the *Harbinger* caught fire in the sectarian press, and Campbell's archenemies made use of it to castigate him. The *Religious Herald* of Richmond, Virginia, wanted to know "On Which Side Is A. Campbell?" It even charged that Campbell's sympathies were really with Fanning rather than Richardson and that he was guilty of making Christianity doctrinal rather than personal. The effort was to set Campbell and Richardson against one another.

For some reason this particular controversy inflamed the imagination of ardent partizans at the two extremes on either side of Richardson, and the discussion spread to Disciple magazines all over the brotherhood. W. S. Russell wrote a series of articles, in the Illinois *Christian Sentinel*, claiming Richardson as a kindred spirit, as he espoused an extreme "spiritualism." Benjamin Franklin, literalist editor of the *American Christian Review*, took sides with Fanning and hurled some very rough language in Richardson's direction.

Although he published nothing in which he singled out Franklin by name, he did write an article repudiating his affinity to Russell's way of thinking. "I thought it necessary for me to censure Bro. Russell," he wrote to Philip S. Fall, "as my name had become unwarrantably associated with his speculations. I have endeavored to do it mildly, however, for he is a young man of piety and ability and I wish we could save him to the cause."

At this point, Campbell decided to curb his associate editor. So for the September issue of the *Harbinger*, he wrote an article entitled "Christianity the True Philosophy," in which he said, quite pointedly: "We do not approve of Philosophical disquisitions of any sort being presented to our readers in our monthly bills of fare. And as little do we approve of placing *faith* and *philosophy* in any real or formal antagonism." He therefore requested that Bacon's *Novum Organum* and Locke's *Essay* be laid on the shelf. "At least let them repose for one lunar month."

Richardson was sorely distressed as he reflected, "I was only enforcing . . . his own excellent and correct teachings in the Christian System." And Fanning did exactly what Richardson feared: he triumphantly reprinted Campbell's article in full.

Campbell's article also gave encouragement to "those editors who were busy circulating every species of calumny" against him, Richardson continued. Not only so, but Campbell "quietly suffered this to go on for months with only one or two slight and very imperfect corrections." Still, he did not hold any ill will toward his senior editor. "Now, do not understand me, Brother Fall," he wrote to his friend, "as *blaming Brother C. for all this or any of it*. I know that influences were thrown artfully around him, at the time, by which his jealousy was excited and his judgment perverted, so that *no assurances on my part seemed to have any effect upon him*."

Fanning himself, on a trip to the North, stopped at Bethany for the special purpose of seeking to turn Mr. Campbell against Dr. Richardson. (Campbell had not recognized this purpose at the time, but a few years later, writing to P. S. Fall on Jan. 4, 1860, he stated that Fanning had made this call "for the especial purpose of creating hostility" in Campbell's mind toward Richardson.) The outcome was that the senior editor moved to censure his associate editor even more severely than at first: "We are told that our custom is to publish both

sides of all our controversies. This is true of all controversies in which I am one party. But this extends not to
every contributor to the Harbinger, nor even to associate
editors." Although subordinated to a footnote, the reprimand was not inconspicuous!

Richardson was discredited. He was hurt most by the
fact that the true Disciple position, as he understood it,
had been publicly denounced, and that by Campbell himself. He refused, however, to enter into controversy with
the aged leader of the reformation. There was, therefore,
but one thing for him to do: resign from the *Harbinger*.
This he did, announcing his withdrawal in the December
number.

There were many who felt that a grave injustice had
been done. One of these, J. A. Butler, wrote to Editor
Bates of the *Evangelist*, published at Fort Madison, Iowa,
that the news of Richardson's resignation from the *Millennial Harbinger* "will murk the spirits of multiplied
thousands." Declaring that Robert Richardson was
among the noblest and ablest early Reformers, he went
on to say that a purer man did not live, "one who would
adorn the most refined society on earth, . . . one whose
luminous light has lamped the feet of thousands of Zion's
children." A grave loss had been sustained by his resignation. "We sorrow much that that man of God has said
to the readers of the *Harbinger*, Fare-thee-well!" Why,
he wanted to know, should "this meek, humble, refined
and pious man" lay down his pen in an hour of such
great need? As he saw the matter, to have Richardson's
name stricken from the list of religious writers "would
be like the going down of the sun on a wintry day!"

Declaring that the situation created "a *crisis* with the Reformation," Butler appealed to Richardson not to withdraw "in the hottest of the fight," after battling so courageously through twenty-eight years in the ranks of the reformation.

It was a sobering experience for Richardson. "The faithful discharge of what I felt to be a duty," he wrote in answer to Butler's open letter, "has brought upon me the most bitter and unrelenting hostility in the form of misquotation, misrepresentation, and personal and professional detraction." He went on to make, for him, an unusually gloomy observation: "Such is the unsettled condition of men's minds, that, it seems to me, scarcely any truth can be presented without being immediately laid hold of by some extremist, and carried away to a false and improper issue." Nevertheless, this bitter experience did not move him from his ground: "I have never, for one moment, thought of withdrawing any aid that I could render to the great and blessed cause in which we are engaged."

To Philip Fall, the tired doctor confided: "But disappointments seem to have clustered around me of late, and I have been a good deal discouraged in regard to the College, and I would feel so in relation to the future of the reformation itself, did I not know that the Lord reigns and that he will not suffer his truth to fail."

When, in addition to the trouble in the *Harbinger*, and concurrently with it, persecution of Richardson arose in the college as well, the doctor found himself beset behind and before.

Following the clue given by the University of Virginia, some of the trustees of Bethany College felt that the ideal pattern of a college or university made provision for the president and professors to live upon the college campus. They hoped in the not too distant future to build adequate faculty housing to realize this ideal; but meantime, an approximation of it could be reached by requiring all faculty members at least to live in the village of Bethany. Professor Richardson, with his home at the top of a high hill, across the Buffalo, lived two miles away.

On many occasions during the past two years, both Pendleton and Campbell had urged the doctor to move his family to Bethany so he could be nearer the college. He had been willing enough to do this. The long hours on horseback and the toll charges on the turnpike were both strong inducements. But he could not find a house. As he wrote to Reuben Coleman, an old friend and a reliable trustee: "All my efforts were fruitless. Bro. Campbell & Bro. Pendleton own all the land round Bethany. Neither will sell an acre or two where a pleasant residence could be built. No ground is to be purchased except some refuse lots in the village of Bethany which Bro. Campbell has still on hand and for which he demands a high price." Having just climbed out of debt, he was not inclined to go back in again anyway. When he looked about for a house to rent, he could find nothing that would even begin to accommodate his large family.

Both Pendleton and Campbell knew all this. He was, therefore, taken by surprise and completely off his guard

179

when on July 3, 1857, upon entering Steward's Inn on the day of the meeting of the Board of Trustees, he was encountered by Dr. J. P. Robison, a comparatively new trustee, who hailed him boisterously, in the presence of a large crowd of students and strangers.

"The Board is going to make you come to Bethany," he said. "We have passed a resolution to that effect. You will have to come. Some of the trustees," he went on recklessly, "say you won't stand for it, but I know you will say that it's all right."

Professor Richardson was almost too startled to reply, but he did manage to say, "Certainly, Doctor, the Board have a right to pass what resolutions they think proper and I think it very proper that they should make all the Faculty come and live on the College premises and furnish them with suitable dwellings." Richardson then expressed a desire to see the resolution and having been given a copy, Dr. Robison joined the other trustees, who were just then gathering, and they passed on into the meeting room, leaving the professor alone.

"Under the circumstances," Richardson continued, in his letter to Trustee Coleman, "I confess, I felt myself not only very much *surprised* but very much *annoyed*." When he looked at the resolution, this is what he read:

> On motion of Dr. Robison, Resolved that the Professors of the College be and they are hereby required to reside in Bethany or its immediate vicinity, and that the new residence of Professor Richardson is out of the vicinity of Bethany as intended by this resolution. . . . Dr. Richardson is requested to comply with this resolution as soon as practicable.

Richardson was stunned. "I confess that upon reading these resolutions a very unpleasant train of reflections and conjectures arose in my mind," he wrote. "Their terms were *imperative*. There had not been shown the slightest recognition of those *official courtesies* which are usually observed in such cases."

There was not a single kindly word acknowledging his past sacrificial services to the institution. "I have met my classes regularly, attending carefully the meeting of the Faculty and faithfully attended to my full share, *to say the least*, of all the business of the College." He confided: "For *sixteen* years I have not been detained *two days* by sickness, and I have not been absent *a single week* from College, except once when my father lay on his dying bed, at which time I was absent about a week. When others were absent, I have attended to their classes for them in addition to my own without any extra compensation. During a large portion of the time, I met Mr. Campbell's morning class for weeks every morning at 8 o'clock, even in the depths of winter, during his long absences from home." His relations with both faculty and students had been entirely friendly and harmonious.

What could be in the mind of the trustees? Did someone want his job? Was someone determined to ride roughshod over realities to get his preconceived notion of an ideal housing pattern? If the trustees were motivated by a desire to have the professors with the students as much as possible, he could certainly qualify on that point.

"I have never on any occasion suffered the distance of my residence to interfere in the slightest degree with my College duties. Indeed it has caused me to spend more time at the College than I would otherwise have done, as when my duties required me to be there early in the morning & also in the evening I have generally remained during the entire day rather than be at the trouble of returning home and coming down again." Moreover, his medical practice took him often into student rooms. "As I am called on often for medical visits and advice, I am often in the rooms of the students both in the Inn and the village—oftener, indeed, far more than any other member of the Faculty." As for entertaining students in his own home, he could qualify on that count, too! "The distance of my residence too, so far from being an obstacle to social intercourse, is on the contrary conducive to it. It is but a pleasant walk for the students to my house. They come out for recreation in parties almost every day. They spend more time in social intercourse with me and my family than they would if I lived in the village."

If the resolution was intended as a means to better discipline of the students, the trustees were harboring an erroneous idea as to its effectiveness.

It is not the location of a man's house that will give him a knowledge of what is going on, but eyes to see and ears to hear. . . . I have constantly from the beginning brought to the notice of the Faculty *more cases of discipline than any other member*, and . . . I have *often* been enabled to lay before the Faculty the facts and occurrences in the *College* and the *village* with which those living in the *immediate vicinity* of the college were wholly ignorant.

Why had he been singled out by name in this resolution? The president himself lived three-quarters of a mile away from the college! "Why single me out as if

I were the only one so placed? . . . What am I to think of this proceeding? Is it a thoughtless exercise of power? Is it a scheme to put me from my position? Or is it a mere whim or favorite motion which some wish to carry out irrespective of consequences?" Thoughts similar to the foregoing ones extracted from Richardson's letter to Reuben Coleman must have raced through his mind during those tense moments following his encounter with Dr. Robison.

Meantime, student talk was buzzing, and with the talk their resentment was gathering momentum. When Dr. Richardson appeared, they thronged around him. They were especially angry at Dr. Robison. They planned, they said, to hold an indignation meeting. He urged them not to do anything, and they were quieted after a while by the pleadings of some of their number who asked respect for the doctor's wishes.

Professor Richardson went on to his room to write a reply to the board that very same day, sending it into the meeting by Alexander Campbell, Jr., who read it:

JULY 3, 1857

TO THE BOARD OF TRUSTEES OF BETHANY COLLEGE,

The Board of Trustees having . . . requested the undersigned to conform to this arrangement at as early a period as practicable, the undersigned feels himself in duty bound to state that he is unconscious of having failed in any respect whatever in the discharge of his *official duties* in consequence of the *distance* of his family residence from the college. It imposes upon him, indeed, much additional toil and expense, as he is obliged to travel in consequence during the session at least 1200 miles which at the rate of 30 miles per day occupies 40 days of time unprofitably expended, but he has never failed to encounter cold and storm and bad roads, to meet his classes punctually, to attend all meetings of the Faculty, and in all respects to promote to the extent of his ability the interests of the Institution, and if it is the judgment of the Board that the distance of his residence from the College has, in any respect, interfered with the faithful discharge of his duties, he begs leave to say that it has been entirely misinformed upon the subject.

He would further state that the question of his removal to Bethany Village has been frequently presented to him, and that . . . it has very *naturally* received full and mature consideration.

Candor obliges him to say, . . . that the circumstances of his family will not permit him to remove to the village of Bethany or the immediate vicinity of the College.

Under these circumstances, but one course remains to the undersigned. . . .

He, therefore, most respectfully tenders to the Board his *immediate resignation* of the chair which he has heretofore occupied in the institution.

R. RICHARDSON

His action took the board so much by surprise that they found themselves passing a new resolution, to constitute "the President, Faculty, J. C. Campbell, C. Tarr, A. F. Ross, and J. H. Pendleton a committee to fill the vacancy by reappointing Dr. Richardson." It was a sobered committee that waited upon the professor shortly afterward. Explanations were given, apologies were made. The doctor was begged to remain. But the command that he move into Bethany was not altered.

The ruffled doctor was not much inclined to reconsider. James Fall, the son of Philip S. Fall of Kentucky, came to him privately, however, and succeeded where the official committee had failed. Fall urged him to consider the state of mind that Campbell was in at the time and to reflect upon the injury which the college and the reformation cause would suffer as a result of his leaving. Richardson could not bear even to think of that, and rather than incur the possibility he determined to make any sacrifice of his own feelings and interests. He decided to reaccept the appointment.

Even then, an effort was made "by tale bearing and other means, to excite Brother Campbell to personal hostility" against Richardson and prevent him from agreeing to his reappointment. Richardson undertook to convince Campbell that there were no grounds for the stories, a task by no means easy when it is remembered that Campbell was then in the most antagonistic phase of the controversy over the series on "Faith *versus* Philosophy." To make sure that his case would get a just hearing in some quarters at least, he explained matters to some of the leading trustees. So at length he was re-elected. To return under such circumstances was a great humiliation to him.

At about this time a Mr. Wendel moved from Bethany to Wheeling, making his property available. Richardson arranged to purchase it (the present Beta House) for $2,500 and undertook the task of crowding his large family into it.

He had supposed that Campbell would be mollified by his compliance with an old request of his and Pendleton's and with the imperative order of the trustees. He was mistaken. Campbell continued to disparage him in the *Harbinger*—among other things, accusing him of teaching the "Spirit alone" theory.

It did not add to his peace of mind when the college engaged Professor J. D. Pickett to teach modern languages without being able to find him a house. Pickett had to leave his family in Kentucky! Meantime, Bethphage was standing empty! Irritated and harassed by editors and trustees, and bedeviled by misunderstandings and misrepresentations, the doctor confronted his duties of the new term in a gray mood, and the year wore on into winter.

On Friday, December 11, 1857, at about two o'clock in the morning, the main college building was discovered to be on fire. Supposed to have been started by an incendiary, the blaze was so far advanced by this time that nothing could be saved. Furnishings, patiently gathered museum, apparatus, the finest library in Virginia, and the building itself—all perished. Students and faculty members, held at bay by the inferno, stood back in agonizing helplessness. Alexander Campbell rushed over from the mansion, and as he saw a large portion of the labor of his seventy years dissolve into ashes, his slumbering brain leaped fully awake to its accustomed vigor. Even while the fire was still burning, he inspired his teachers and his students to plan to rebuild immediately.[5]

Classes resumed the very next day, crowding into Steward's Inn. The following Monday, December 14, the trustees met in emergency session and took swift measures to rebuild more nobly than the last. President Campbell and Vice-President Pendleton were authorized to do what they were already planning, to take to the field in an effort to raise $50,000 at once. Campbell, Pendleton, and Richardson were appointed a committee to prepare a financial appeal to the college constituency, asking for immediate aid in re-erecting the college buildings and refurnishing its library and laboratory.[6]

Trustees Curran, John C. Campbell, and Ross and Professors Pendleton, Richardson, and Pickett were appointed a committee to draw up plans for new college buildings, to prepare estimates and specifications, and to receive bids from contractors.

President Campbell and Vice-President Pendleton left at once on an extensive tour to raise funds. Then fell upon Richardson the task of ordering scientific equipment to replenish the destroyed laboratories, planning with the building committee, teaching his own, Campbell's, and Pendleton's classes in the crowded Steward's Inn, and the administrative responsibilities of acting president and bursar. As these tasks devolved upon him, added as they were to the busy life he normally lived, and to the almost overbearing weight of misunderstanding and hostility which the Fanning controversy and the faculty housing resolution had provoked, not to mention the gloom occasioned by the physical disaster to the college, Robert Richardson will perhaps be forgiven if he did not respond very cheerfully.

Chapter XIV

"WITH HEARTS OVERFLOWING"

Bethany, in the early months of 1858, held fewer charms for Robert Richardson than it had in all the twenty-two years of his residence there. He was living in the village under duress, away from Bethphage, in a house that had run him into debt and whose amortization stretched far into the future. His resignation from the editorial staff of the *Millennial Harbinger* virtually amounted to dismissal, as well as being a step which automatically reduced his annual income by $300;[1] in addition, with both the president and vice-president away, he was playing again his familiar role, without additional pay, bearing the burdens of both. Worst of all, Alexander Campbell, in whose very shadow he had lived and whose confidence he had shared for nearly a quarter of a century, was estranged from him.

Toward the end of the year, he wrote his friend Philip Fall:

> With my income reduced, and involved in a debt for a house, a burden most ungenerously laid upon me through the overbearing disposition of one or two members of the board, and seeing my children ranging up and down the creek—coming into contact with injurious influences in the village, and without any prospect of my being able to send them abroad to school, I was in such a frame of mind that when, without any application, directly or indirectly on my part, Kentucky University offered me a place, it seemed that the Lord had designed me for another part. I felt it my duty to go.[2]

Bacon College, which had been founded at George-town, Kentucky, in 1836 as the first college of the Disciples and which later moved to Harrodsburg, had closed its doors on June 14, 1850.[3] Dr. Samuel Hatch, a member of the old faculty, continued for the next five years to conduct a small high school in the college building. Meantime, the trustees were struggling unsuccessfully to reopen the institution. By October 22, 1855, John B. Bowman, an alumnus of Bacon College, had conceived the idea of raising a university on the ruins of the old college and had called a meeting of the trustees to approve the plan. They caught his enthusiasm and voted to begin raising funds at once. By November 7, 1856, an endowment of $100,000 had been subscribed. Mr. Bowman himself, as time ran on, raised an average of $1,000 per day for 150 days.

> A meeting of the donors was held the first Wednesday of May, 1857, to decide on future plans. John Allen Gano was the chairman of the meeting. As a result of their deliberations a committee of seven was appointed to present to the trustees of Bacon College suggested amendments to the charter and to secure the enactment of these by the legislature.

It was decided to change the name to "Kentucky University." The legislature granted a new charter embodying the changes desired, and it "was approved by the trustees of Bacon College, February 2, 1858"; subsequently it was approved by the newly formed board of curators of Kentucky University.

The Board of Curators of Kentucky University met in an official capacity on February 4, 1858, to constitute a faculty.[4] Meantime, preliminary discussions had been going on to feel out prospective faculty members, and Robert Richardson had received such a "feeler." There was general talk in Kentucky about the personnel of the university. Alexander Campbell and W. K. Pendleton ran into this rumor when they reached that state on their tour to finance the rebuilding of Bethany College, as is shown by a paragraph from a letter written by Pendleton to Richardson from Macedonia, Kentucky, on January 29, 1858:

> I am at Bro. Wm. McKinney's. He is delicate. He says it is out of the question for Bacon College to open next fall. It is commonly said that Prof. Milligan has been elected President and R. Richardson and Prof. White, Profs.—and some say it is the determination of some of the Board to break down Bethany. This I hope is not so. But of this more when I see you.[5]

The February 4, 1858, meeting of the Board of Curators elected Robert Milligan, of Bethany College, president and professor of biblical literature and ethics; Professor John H. Neville, of Christian University, to the chair of ancient languages; Charles L. Loos, president of Eureka College, to the chair of belles-lettres; and Robert Richardson was made professor of natural science and vice-president of the faculty, at a salary of $1,500 per year. However, the curators directed their Committee on Correspondence to inform Milligan and Richardson that, due to the financial condition of the new university, and in consideration of the calamity that had recently befallen Bethany College, their services would not be required before the 1859-60 session.[6]

Shortly after this meeting, the Richardson mail contained the following letter:[7]

HARRODSBURG, KENTUCKY
FEBRUARY 8th, 1858

MY DEAR BRO. RICHARDSON,

I take great pleasure in informing you that at the recent meeting of the Board of Curators of Kentucky University, you were unamiously elected to fill the Chair of Physical Science and appointed also Vice President of the Institution.

A large majority of the Board were present, representing the interest of the friends and Donors of the Enterprise, and I would say, that we feel assured that your acceptance of the position will give great satisfaction, not only to the Board of Curators, but to the Kentucky brethren generally, and we do earnestly hope that you will find it consistent with your interests and sense of duty to give us an assurance of your acceptance at as early a date as possible. We do cordially believe that there is in the future of our Enterprise, more promise of unselfishness to the Cause of Education and Christianity than in that of any other in the Mississippi Valley, and that our brethren generally are turning their eyes to it, with more pride and hope than to any other among them. In view of the financial affairs of the Institution and of the calamity at Bethany and our sympathy with that College, the Board deemed it inexpedient to attempt a full organization of Ky. University before September 1859. The proposition to you is, that your appointment will take effect at that time, with a salary of $1500.00 till $100,000 of Endowment fund is invested. Hoping that this also will be acceptable to you,

I remain your Bro. in Christ,

JNO. B. BOWMAN.

To this Dr. Richardson made formal reply on February 15, 1858, the next day after receiving it! "Having already maturely considered the questions involved in this contemplated movement, it only remains for me to say in reply that I feel grateful to the Board of Curators for this mark of their confidence and that I frankly accept the chair which they have tendered me according to the terms of your letter."

In April, when Campbell and Pendleton came back from their long tour in the East and South, they undertook to convince him that Kentucky University could not live and that his and Milligan's going there would be a serious blow to Bethany, which, in its critical hour, it might not be able to survive. Richardson perceived that a remarkable change had taken place in the lately estranged Mr. Campbell. It was with joy that he noted: "Brother Campbell is very well since his return from his long tour, and speaks as well as I ever knew him to do."

Richardson reminded Campbell of his recent antagonism toward him over the Fanning matter. To his amazement, Campbell seemed to have forgotten all about it, as though it had all happened in a dream. He promised that everything should be made right. His attitude became and continued to be as friendly as in the olden days.[8]

Campbell was as good as his word. The *Millennial Harbinger* for May, 1858, carried a full apology. Regarding Richardson's views in the recent series on "Faith *versus* Philosophy," he said: "These are just the views which we have held and advocated, and I know not how the misstatement above referred to could have occurred, unless that writing the article away from home, I had not an opportunity of examining Bro. R's essays, and had probably before my mind some of those misquotations and misrepresentations of which he has complained and which we have regretted to see in some of our western periodicals."

In the next issue of his magazine Campbell administered a sound spanking to President Fanning:

> He persists in endeavoring to make the impression on the public mind, that Dr. Richardson and certain other brethren whom he names, are teaching, as he says "unmixed and unblushing infidelity." This charge he affects to sustain by a few brief extracts from their writings. These extracts do not at all sustain Pres't F.'s assertion, and we wish to say that we consider [his attacks] an outrage upon both editorial and Christian courtesy. . . .
>
> As to Bro. Richardson, I am perfectly familiar with his sentiments on all questions involved, and I can assure Pres't F. that he does him the grossest injustice. . . . Others who can judge of the "meaning of words" as well as Pres't Fanning, do not find in Bro. Richardson's essays the slightest ground for Pres't F's charge, and invectives, nor will the intelligent brethren justify or sanction his reckless assertions.

In a letter to Philip Fall on January 4, 1860, he confessed: "I have, . . . ever since my late tour to Mississippi, viewed Elder Fanning as intent on war with us under some pretense or other. And I still must regard him as hostile to Bethany, and, indeed, I know not why—or wherefore, unless an unsanctified ambition lurks within him."

Alexander Campbell's forthright statement cleared the air. Furthermore, he immediately insisted that both Richardson and Milligan return to the staff of the *Millennial Harbinger*. This would be the surest way of putting down the rumors which had grown out of the affair. Richardson recognized this and readily accepted.[9]

Restored to grace, Richardson was now sorry that he had accepted the post at Kentucky University. At the same time, he was afraid that the happy sunlight of Campbell's returning clarity of mind might once more recede into the shadows. "If Brother Campbell were left to himself, I should have no fears," he wrote to Philip Fall. Limping indecisively between the two sides, he carried on his work for the remainder of the term without giving notice to the Board of Trustees that he intended to resign, although his acceptance at Kentucky University was an open secret.

During the next few months, Professor Richardson helped Bowman with the formation of the new Kentucky institution. Charles Louis Loos, having declined his appointment in order, interestingly enough, to return to Bethany College as professor of modern languages, Richardson nominated another of his own students for the position. This was Robert Graham, who was then preaching in Fayetteville, Arkansas. Richardson wrote convincingly to him, and Graham consented to come.

Meantime, the cornerstone had been ceremoniously laid for the new building at Bethany College on May 31, 1858.[10] The building which emerged was a crown of collegiate Gothic architecture, along the lines of the University of Glasgow, set upon the brow of the hill. It was a two- and three-story structure, having 420 feet of continuous front, with a 320-foot open corridor running the entire length of the central section in the rear, lifting at center a lofty tower clock and spire 122 feet into the air. The right wing, known as Society Hall, was completed first and was ready for occupancy in 1858. Work progressed toward Commencement Hall at the left wing, which was built in 1873. In 1862 construction was halted when the entire length of the building was enclosed and roofed, but the inside was not completely finished until the end of the decade. The entire project, up to 1868, had cost $80,000. Toward this amount the Campbell-Pendleton tours in 1857 and 1858 realized about $30,000.[11]

The mortgage on his Bethany house worried Richardson almost unendurably. This, together with his unannounced plans to go to Kentucky, moved him to petition the trustees, on July 1, 1858, that he be permitted to return to his farm.

The board responded by a motion stating that "the permission desired is for the present granted," but, they said, "in view of the expected absence of the President and Vice-President during the coming year, the Trustees would be pleased if Professor Richardson could so arrange his private affairs, as to remain at the College and give it his undivided attention."

When the Board of Trustees met on August 14, 1858, it demanded to know what Professors Richardson and Milligan were planning to do about their rumored appointment to Kentucky University, and legislated that "they be requested to notify said Committee by the first of December next, whether they accept or decline said appointments."

As the date of the board's ultimatum approached, the doctor was tossed on a sea of uncertainty. Could he disappoint Bowman at Kentucky University? Should he put himself again in the power of those who had just exercised their authority over him so cruelly? Would his going actually injure Bethany? With Campbell in his declining years, he wished earnestly that the support going into Kentucky had been concentrated at Bethany to prevent the expectation of Campbell's enemies that the college would not survive him. His attachments in Bethany were like those of an old and well-rooted tree. He prayed for the right way.

The two men resigned December 1, 1858, and the board received their letters with "cordial acknowledgements for the efficiency and ability with which for a series of years" they had "discharged the duties incumbent upon them" as members of the faculty.

There were at that time about thirty students from Kentucky enrolled in Bethany College. As soon as the resignation became public, all of them made an evening pilgrimage to Bethphage and, through a selected spokesman, formally welcomed the doctor to Kentucky. Quelling the storm of conflicting emotions within his breast, he cleared his throat and made them a charming reply. Mrs. Richardson asked the young men into the house and, with characteristic grace and hospitality, served refreshments to the group.

As associate editor of the *Millennial Harbinger* again, Richardson wrote numerous articles and series of articles for his beloved publication. None was closer to the central issues of Protestantism than his series on "Christian Unity," which began in February, 1859. Discussing Jesus' great intercessory prayer in the seventeenth chapter of John, he said that its application had been "totally misunderstood; its fulfilment wholly overlooked," that it had "no direct reference, whatever, to the subject of an outward or visible union among Christians." He distinguished sharply between *union* and *unity*. "By Christian UNITY, we understand *a spiritual Oneness with Christ;* by Christian UNION, *an avowed agreement and co-operation of Christians with each other.*" We must not mistake unity for union, and certainly there can be no genuine union without unity. This means that unity will come on the ground of Christian liberty, or that it will not come at all.

This being the case, Richardson told his readers that the coming of Christian unity did not depend upon getting all Christians aligned to the mechanics of the Disciple pattern. "After all, it is not to be denied that there are 'Christians among the sects,' and that piety, philanthropy and lovely works—the precious buds and blossoms and fruits of true religion, are manifested, more or less, in almost all religious parties." In contrast to this, dissension is already beginning to appear among the Disciples, who, ironically, came into being to plead for Christian unity. The thoughtful Disciple "perceives, also, with surprise, that there are differences amongst his own followers, and that his serpent [referring to Aaron's rod before Pharaoh, Exod. 7:11-12], which he fondly hoped would have swallowed up the rest, is more likely to add to the number a brood of its own."

One reason for this internal division and for the increasingly sectarian character of the reformation—which arose to end all sects—was that too many of its adherents were crusading for an outward organizational and literal pattern of *union* instead of an inner, spiritual *unity*. Disunion, in itself, of course, may do much to destroy unity. Hence the divided condition of Protestantism is to be deplored; but external union, by its insistence upon legalistic uniformity, may become just as fatally divisive. The real test of the whole matter is whether there is peace; for the existence of peace "in a feeble or doubtful manner, indicates that the Spirit of Christ is present only in small and defective measure."

The associate editor also, in January of the same year, paid his respects, in passing, to a new debate then raging over "soul sleeping." This was the belief that between mortal death and immortality there was an interim in which the soul slept until awakened on the judgment day. Sides lined up for and against this issue, and the argument was furious. Richardson said, sharply, that this was another instance of divisive speculations which were far wide of the mark. Essential Christianity was not interested in such issues. He added, somewhat humorously, that although there was "a superabundance of 'soul-sleeping' in *this* world, there are, it seems, some who are again advocating its existence in the *next*." Christians ought to be about the tasks of the living, and should awake the slumbering, rather than add to their numbers! "It is not a greater extent of revelation that we need, but a better acquaintance with what we have—a more earnest, sincere and heartfelt trust in the Author of this revelation. . . . Christian ignorance gives scope for Christian faith, but knowledge, whether real or pretended, puffs up, too often, the heart with vain self-confidence and conceit."

At the 1859 commencement, Bethany College conferred the honorary degree of Master of Arts upon Robert Milligan and Robert Richardson for their long and faithful service.[12] Dr. Richardson had been similarly honored the same spring, much to his delight, by Jefferson College, at Cannonsburg, Pennsylvania,[13] a school which later joined with Washington College to form Washington and Jefferson College. Seven years earlier, the same college had conferred the degree of Doctor of Divinity upon Alexander Campbell.

Vice-President Pendleton, recouping losses and rebuilding confidence, announced: "The vacancies in the Faculty, created by the resignations of Professors Richardson and Milligan . . . have been filled. . . . It will be seen, therefore, that the Faculty of Bethany College is full and complete, composed of Seven Professors, besides an adjunct corps of Assistant Tutors in the various schools."[14]

The *Millennial Harbinger* for October carried a simple and inconspicuous announcement about two of its associate editors: "All communications to R. Richardson and to R. Milligan, after the First of September, should be sent to Harrodsburg, Kentucky."[15]

Robert Richardson's emotions, as he passed through these events uprooting him from the college and the community of which he was so much a part and which was so much a part of him, can best be stated in the words of the "Alma Mater":

199

. . . .

How dear to our hearts,
    Are the scenes of Old Bethany.
God speed Alma Mater,
    And dear old Bethany.

. . . .

High up on the scroll
    Of honor and fame.
Thy sons strong and manly
    Have written thy name.

. . . .

But now we must leave thee
    With hearts overflowing.
Farewell, Alma Mater
    And dear old Bethany!

Chapter XV

A HOUSE DIVIDED

When the Richardson family moved from Bethany in 1859, Nathaniel and Anne did not accompany them. On June 2 of that year Nathaniel had married Anne Mc-Kennon; and, as we have seen, Anne Richardson had previously married J. M. Dunning. In fact, Nathaniel, having attained to some celebrity as a brilliant young lawyer in Wheeling, had been elected to the House of Delegates in the government of the State of Virginia and was just now beginning his first term.

The home in the village that Richardson had purchased under duress was sold to Professor C. L. Loos. Bethphage was turned over to the keeping of Mr. and Mrs. John Stevenson, who now moved from the tenant house into the old family home. Mrs. Stevenson had long been a friend of the family, in earlier years having helped Mrs. Richardson with the work about the house.

Upon arriving in Harrodsburg, Dr. Richardson moved into a home located at the intersection of Lexington and Nicholson roads. A deed dated at Harrodsburg, September 1, 1859, shows that this home was purchased from Elizabeth Morrow for $3,750, of which $1,000 was paid in cash, the balance being covered by notes to be paid within two years. The house was situated on two and a half acres of land. It was a large, well-appointed, American-Gothic dwelling. The grounds were ample, the house sitting in a grove of trees well back from the street; a long walk led up from the highway. Within the house there was a tall, spiral stairway leading to the second and third floors, from the base of which one could see all the way up. To assist Rebekah in the care of this home, colored servants were employed, but not purchased, for Dr. Richardson was strongly opposed to slavery.

Mary and Frances were entered at Daughters College, in Harrodsburg. David was enrolled as a student in Kentucky University, and John in Taylor Academy. Anne had previously attended Piedmont Seminary in Virginia, and Nathaniel had graduated from Bethany College.

Kentucky University opened September 19, 1859. There were 194 students.[1] Professor Robert Richardson published the following departmental description for the School of Physical Science:

> The design of this Department is to give to the student a very thorough and extensive knowledge of the laws, principles, and operations of the material world, organic and inorganic. The daily recitations are accompanied with familiar lectures, and as far as practicable, with a very full course of experiments on all subjects taught.
>
> Special attention is also given to the subject of Practical Analysis, the Laws of Health, the Principles of Agriculture, and the general application of Chemistry to the arts; while the benevolent designs of the Creator in the constitution of nature are kept constantly before the minds of the students.[2]

The course of study and instruction in his school covered the whole range of the then known field of physical science. Textbooks listed were "Olmsted's Natural Philosophy; Silliman's Chemistry; Gray's Botanical Text-Book; Carpenter's Physiology; Agassiz and

Gould's Zoology; Dana's Manual of Mineralogy; Hitchcock's Geology; and Johnson's Agricultural Chemistry."

For this and for all his services as vice-president, as the minutes of the Board of Curators show, Richardson was paid $1,500 the first year. The following year the schedule was revised, and his salary was raised to $1,750, the high-water mark of his whole career; but this improvement in his situation was to be of short duration.

During most of Richardson's first year at Kentucky University, his work was conducted upon the trembling threshold of approaching civil war. When the second term began, the conflict was already under way. Students from his classes enlisted on both sides of the fraternal strife. Tensions tore at the school, enrollment fell off. The second session began with 174 students, an enrollment which was reduced the third term to 113 and the fourth to sixty-two.[3]

Commencement at Bethany College on July 4, 1860, found Robert Richardson at the exercises, where he was seated among the distinguished gentlemen on the platform.[4] His reasons for returning were many. The most important of these was his desire to demonstrate his support of Bethany College and his personal esteem for Campbell. Another was a wish to see the new college building, of which Alexander Campbell had recently said: "Our building is in its whole contour one of the finest I have seen old world or new—of Collegiate Gothic Architecture—It is in good keeping with our Gothic Hills."[5] Then again, he was homesick; and he wanted to see how the Stevensons were getting along at Bethphage.

From the very first, upon reaching a definite decision to go to Kentucky, he had been concerned to keep his removal from being interpreted as a break with Bethany College or with Alexander Campbell. Even after they were in Kentucky, both he and Milligan had offered to continue as associate editors of the *Harbinger*, with or without salary. Although neither of them wanted the extra burden of editorial work, they thought it would tend to promote peace and prevent rivalry between the two institutions.[6]

In the early 1860's a controversy broke out in the brotherhood over "inviting the pious unimmersed to the Lord's Table." Many Disciples, prominent among whom were Moses E. Lard and Benjamin Franklin, ranged themselves on the close-communion side of this issue; others, like Isaac Errett and Robert Richardson, opposed that position.

The close-communion position is briefly but accurately set forth in the following statement by George W. Elley, of Lexington, Kentucky:

> I will state my position in a few words: 1. That the church of God is composed only of those who are avowedly "born again." 2. That none are thus born who have not been immersed in water, upon their public avowal of their faith and repentance. 3. That such, and such only, are citizens of Christ's kingdom; and such are (all other things being equal), lawfully entitled to the ordinances of God's house.[7]

Characteristically, Richardson did not allow himself to be put in a position of countering this extreme with another. He took a position that was moderately liberal:

The discussions . . . have been upon the question of the recognition of unimmersed persons as Christians, and "open communion" is urged upon the ground that the members of the different churches *are* Christians, and therefore *entitled* to intercommunion, and to be *invited* accordingly. This question is here supposed to be discussed and determined by immersed believers in *favor of* all others. Our position is quite different; we neither discuss nor determine this question. We simply leave it to each individual to determine for himself.

It was really, as the close-communion partisans said, an "untaught question." And for this reason, if for no other, the position was illogical and self-contradictory.

These brethren, however, act very inconsistently, when, after declaring it an "untaught question," they then proceed to discuss it, or what is still worse, to *determine* it without discussion, *against* all but immersed believers. . . . In so deciding, they presume to decide two questions, 1st, that *no* unimmersed persons are Christians; 2nd, that all immersed persons are Christians—neither of which propositions can be proved.[8]

Richardson's exact position was that of "informal communion." The unimmersed "are neither invited nor prohibited." Since their exact status is an "untaught question," it must be left to each person. It "is *their* act and not *ours*." Of an advocate of close communion he wanted to know whether this practice of "informal communion" was not quite general among Disciples and whether he was not aware that it was a common occurrence for "members of other religious communities, who happen to be seated amongst our brethren, to partake of the loaf and the cup" as they are passed. Has he "ever heard the individual presiding prohibit the practice, or 'fence the tables' in presbyterian phrase, or [ever] known the church as a body to object to it?"[9]

Isaac Errett, Richardson's personal friend, was upholding the same side of the issue. Answering an inquiry from R. Hawley, he stated that although the Disciple position did not recognize *sects* as being of divine origin, it certainly did recognize "a people of God among these sects." He went on to say:

> We are compelled, therefore, to recognize as Christians many who have been in error on baptism, but who in the *spirit* of obedience are Christians indeed. . . . It will never do to unchristianize those on whose shoulders we are standing, and because of whose previous labors we are enabled to see some truths more clearly than they. . . .
>
> For myself, while fully devoted to our plea, I have no wish to limit and fetter my sympathies and affections to our own people.[10]

Richardson regarded the close-communion stand as bigoted and narrow. Reading the "labored essays intended to build up exclusivism and Pharisaism" among the Disciples, he experienced a deep desire "to expose their sophistries" and defeat their aims. "But I am too much occupied with my labors in the University here, and in the church, to write much at present."[11]

In July, 1861, John Hunt Morgan, the "Thunderbolt of the Confederacy," at the head of 1,200 of the now celebrated "Morgan Raiders," invaded Kentucky from eastern Tennessee, preparatory to Bragg's march into the state. As the raiders roamed about, plundering and destroying, their lightninglike depredations created intense excitement. Men rallied to Morgan's banner by the hundreds.

This time of general disturbance was disastrous to Richardson's personal affairs. On July 8, 1861, he wrote his son Nathaniel, "I have never had so much trouble to obtain the means of defraying my current expenses as during the past few months." He had met financial reverses and difficulties. The university could not pay his salary, and he did not know how he was going to raise the $1,250 which was still due on his house.

By early summer of 1862 it was evident that the conflict in Kentucky would shortly become more bitter and more intense. Richardson feared for his family, and finally decided to take them back to the North. Accordingly, in July of that year, leaving David behind to enter upon the schoolteaching for which he had contracted, he started north with the remainder of the family. Traveling by stagecoach and by rail, he was fortunate enough to get the last train leaving that section for many months. The family was now safe again at Bethphage. The farm was put under the management of his son John, and the doctor prepared to return to Harrodsburg.

But his return was delayed. Shortly after the arrival of the Richardson family at Bethphage, a letter came from Milligan, acquainting them with recent developments in Kentucky:

A few days ago, I thought that our prospects were becoming very flattering. But the recent order of the Government, to draft 300,000 men has produced some excitement in Ky. Many young men will make every possible effort to escape to the Southern Confederacy. And it is now confidently believed, that Morgan will attempt another raid through Ky. for the purpose of gaining recruits. If he be successful, he will gain many more recruits than he did during the last raid. But it is thought that the Union force will soon be strong enough to resist any attempt to invade Ky.[12]

At about the same time a letter from David showed that this son of his had become greatly excited over the war and that he perhaps was thinking of enlisting in the Confederate Army. This news depressed and displeased his father, who replied from Bethphage, August 20, 1862:

DEAR DAVID,

I received your letter a few days ago, and am pleased to learn that your school has increased. I feel under many obligations to Dr. Campbell for the kindness he has shown you. Give my kind regards to him and the family.

I regret much that Ky. has become so much disturbed lately. I heard last evening a report that the Confederate forces had occupied Richmond, Ky. [25 miles south of Lexington]. If this be so I fear there will be little peace in Ky. for some time and that it may be made a great battle ground for the two opposing sections. If you should happen to be drafted you should find a substitute as I would not wish you to engage on either side of this unhappy contest. I am opposed to it altogether, and regret it especially on account of the south which will be totally ruined if it continues much longer. . . . Any one who aids the South in the rebellion aids in her destruction. I regret that you allow yourself to speak so rashly and unjustly of individuals and public measures, in regard to which, you are necessarily an incompetent judge. You will do well to be a quiet observer for a few years and to avoid any expressions of opinions which may make you enemies and can, in no case, subserve a useful purpose.

. . . .

I hope you will confine yourself to business closely and endeavor to improve your pupils and yourself by every means in your power. Avoid political discussions altogether and endeavor to enlarge your knowledge by the study of history and a review of your studies. Try to render full satisfaction to your employers and to gain their confidence by punctuality and attention. I will be glad to hear of your success and wish you to write occasionally to let me know how you are getting on.

Yours affectionately,

R. RICHARDSON.

After the battle of Perryville, on October 8, 1862, the Kentucky University buildings were taken over as a Confederate hospital, and the college retired to the Christian church.[13] Professor Richardson did not return to Harrodsburg for the fall term of 1862. A letter to Nathaniel, written December 7, 1862, shows him still debating whether he would return to Harrodsburg at all. There were only fifty students. He might do it, if he could be sure of getting $400 in cash which he would then be able to credit to the $800 he had borrowed from the school the previous year. His family was in need of a carriage, but he could not even afford $50 for a second-hand vehicle. It was a gloomy and uncertain time. Finally, he decided to wait until the beginning of the second semester, in February, 1863. Meantime, he supervised the farm, practiced medicine, and brooded over the armed strife rending his nation.

The Neotrophian Literary Society in Bethany College, of which Dr. Richardson was a member, invited him to address them, and in November, 1862, he obliged them with a stirring address against war. He told them that Bethany was "a green spot, in the present, amidst the desert waste of political turmoil and civil war." He lamented the bloodshed of former Bethany students who now fought one another on the battlefield. He disparaged military men and the military art: "There seems to me no better evidence of the fact that 'men are but children of a larger growth,' than to see a tall, broad-chested, whiskered individual, making a vain display of a few brass buttons and strips of gold lace with which the tailor has bedecked his clothing." Victory in battle, he continued, is often a matter of "mere animal courage and brutal force," rather than a triumph of genius. The work of the scholar was more important to America's future than the work of the soldier, he said. "It is here then, gentlemen, within these halls, that you are engaged in the most elevated of all employments." But even in such grim times and with very heavy personal anxieties on his mind, the doctor could not resist a pun:

> We are, indeed, most happily located here in the Pan-handle of Virginia. The rest of the State is the pan, and the long narrow strip of land between Ohio and Pa. on which we live, is the handle of the pan. How much better it is to be situated on the handle of the pan, than to be in the pan itself during these "trying" not to say *frying* times![14]

Western Virginia, meantime, moved to dissociate itself from the seceding mother state. Calling a convention at Wheeling on May 14, 1861, it condemned the ordinance of secession. On June 20, following a referendum, the fifty-six elected delegates at Wheeling declared the separation of western from eastern Virginia and set up a provisional government. On November 27 "West Virginia" was chosen to be the name of the new state, and on May 3, 1862, the people ratified the new state constitution. Somewhat more than a year later, on June 20, 1863, the new state was admitted to the Union.

Tensions which split sons and brothers between the two contending armies infused with bitter antagonism the voting which severed one part of Virginia from the other. In this strained situation, Robert Richardson moved in and out among his old neighbors and patients, laboring tirelessly as a peacemaker, a role for which he was peculiarly fitted by talent, training, and temperament.

With regard to David, his worst fears were shortly realized. His son joined Morgan's Raiders. When David entered the conflict, Richardson wrote brokenheartedly to his friend Philip Fall, as though he had suffered a bereavement. Fall replied from Nashville, on December 13, 1862. A part of his letter follows:

> I agree with you that this war is a crime—because it might easily have been avoided, had the powers that be so willed. Allow me to say that we know how to feel for the bereavement you have been called upon to suffer in anticipation; and if at any time your son, who is possibly at Murfreesboro at this moment, should be in our city either sick or wounded, or a prisoner, we hope to be able to take him to our house and treat him as our own. A battle is imminent. Skirmishes are taking place almost daily and the Federal losses in prisoners as well as killed and wounded have been very heavy within the last two weeks.[15]

This was painful consolation. Though deeply appreciated, it was impotent to assuage his grief. It was only a little more than a year and a half later, on July 5, 1864, that David fell in battle with Morgan's Raiders at Lebanon, Kentucky, in the twenty-second year of his life. Afterward, Richardson repressed his sorrow, closing the door upon that part of his mind. Never again, even once, did he mention David's name in the family circle.[16] Rebekah, whose sympathies were with the Confederacy, and whose affection for David was correspondingly augmented, was crushed.

In January, 1863, the doctor undertook the hazardous return to Kentucky. Immediately upon reaching Harrodsburg, he wrote his family, on February 8, 1863, addressing the letter to his son John:

> I did not get to Harrodsburg until Friday evening owing to the railroad trains failing to make connections. I find the friends here generally well and glad to see me. I have commenced my labors today at the University, this being the first day of the second term. I have concluded to take boarding at Mrs. Arnold's as the most convenient place. A number of students are boarding with her; also an Episcopal clergyman. She has her son George with her who was badly wounded in the skirmish at Cynthiana last fall. He was one of Morgan's band and is lying now very low, not expected to recover. There are about 54 students on the University Register and more expected.
>
> I forgot in coming away to tell you that the pork in the brine in the smokehouse ought to be hung up. If not done you had best hang it up at once and keep up a smoke every day for two or three weeks. *Make as little heat as possible.* Use hickory wood and do not pile it up so as to make any blaze, but fix it so that it will burn very slowly and make merely smoke. Attend to it frequently and be careful to keep the fire in the middle of the smoke house. You can take some of the broom twine I gave you and after making a hole in each ham and shoulder, push the cord through. Hang them up *with the shanks downward*, and give the cords a good hold in the meat and skin so that it will not cut out. In hanging the pieces up, do not let them touch each other. . . .
>
> I hope you have got the stacks into the barn and the other hauling done before this, as it is now thawing again. Be careful to remember my directions about the sheep—keep the colts in the barn yard and let the sheep always have hay in the racks before the barn, and their corn regularly.
>
> Write about every two weeks and let me know all that is done and how things are.

Tell Eddie and Emma that they must write. Alf. Curry was glad to hear from Eddie and to receive the apples. Bob was greatly pleased to get the 2 big apples from Willy. I sent out the presents for Henry and Will White but have not seen them yet. Mrs. Curry and family are well and the folks generally.

Dr. Richardson remained in Kentucky only until the close of the semester. The resources of the university were shattered and the students dispersed to the war. Frugal, and anxious to be a burden to no one, Richardson turned his face to the North and joined his family at his beloved Bethphage. Fortunately, he had been able to dispose of his Harrodsburg property to a businessman, a Mr. Foster, at a financial loss of only $250. He received $1,500 in cash and two notes for $1,000 each, to be paid within eighteen months.

On February 16, 1864, the main building of Kentucky University was destroyed by fire. Plunged into great distress and uncertainty by this blow, the curators considered what to do—whether to rebuild in Harrodsburg or to start new in Louisville or Covington or to accept the long-standing invitation of Transylvania University to move to Lexington, in which case it was agreed that Transylvania's property and the government of the university would be transferred to the curators of Kentucky University. The curators, after many months of discussion, decided to accept Transylvania's offer. Meantime, classes were being held in the Harrodsburg Christian church and in a neighboring building.[17]

President Milligan wrote Richardson repeatedly, urging him to return, but the doctor would not budge. He had come home to Bethany, and there he intended to remain.

Chapter XVI

THE "MEMOIRS OF ALEXANDER CAMPBELL"

Bethany College, in the fall of 1865, was climbing out of a valley of small enrollments which had almost, but not quite, closed her doors during the war years. She rebounded to normalcy with great rapidity. In the twenty-fifth year of her life, this institution now proudly boasted the following representation of her alumni in the professions: fifteen physicians, thirty-four teachers, thirty-five lawyers, forty-seven farmers and planters, and 108 ministers.[1]

In July of this year Robert Richardson was again elected to the Board of Trustees, and in the fall he resumed his teaching as professor of natural philosophy, chemistry, and natural history. Alexander Campbell was still president, but he had been inactive for several years; throughout most of the war he was mercifully oblivious to the ordeal of his country. Richardson's colleagues at this time were W. K. Pendleton, vice-president and professor of mental, moral, and political philosophy; Charles Louis Loos, professor of ancient languages and literature; and B. W. Johnson, professor of mathematics and astronomy.

Pendleton, who was now not only acting president of the college but also editor of the *Millennial Harbinger*, used this organ to announce the doctor's return:

> We congratulate the friends of the College on the return of Dr. R. Richardson to the Faculty. He was one of the *first* Faculty ever formed in Bethany College, and has been engaged

as a teacher for a quarter of a century. He has won and justly deserves a place of highest distinction among us as an educator, and is especially eminent in the Department which is now committed to him in Bethany College.[2]

Richardson's salary during this first year was $1,000, while those of Johnson, Loos, and Pendleton were $1,-500, $2,000, and $2,500 respectively. The following year he was advanced to $1,500 and given additional responsibility as curator of the museum. Significantly, he was "excused from living in town."

In March, 1866, Alexander Campbell brought his earthly pilgrimage to a close. His last public appearance was before the Bethany church on February 11. He had entered the pulpit intending to preach. Noting the feebleness of his voice when he attempted to read the opening hymn, Pendleton dissuaded him from trying to continue, whereupon Richardson took charge. The doctor's sermon that day was on the third chapter of 2 Peter. He dwelt upon the divine promise of "new heavens and a new earth, wherein dwelleth righteousness." Mr. Campbell gave close and rapt attention. Later the venerable patriarch assisted at the Communion and in the ordination of two additional elders in the Bethany church.[3]

Thereafter, Campbell was confined to his home. He sank rapidly. Dr. Richardson, as family physician, attended him in this illness, reporting somewhat clinically, "He had some cough, some oppression and slight, irregular pains in the chest, a frequent and feverish pulse." Now and then he engaged his old companion in conversation about the cause that lay upon the heart of both. One of the last of these conversations concerned a proposed meeting of Baptists and Disciples in Richmond, Virginia, to discuss the possibilities of uniting the two bodies. This news pleased Campbell. "There was never any sufficient reason," said he, "for a separation between us and the Baptists. We ought to have remained one people, and to have labored together to restore the primitive faith and practice."[4]

Campbell lingered on the threshold of death. Richardson, as his attending physician, reported: "At times a brightening gleam of renewed intellectual power. Again a wandering—he was away from home—anxious to be home; often asking those around him when they would start for home; yet gently acquiescing in the reply of 'presently.' "[5]

This continued until fifteen minutes before twelve o'clock on March 4, 1866, when the venerable Reformer parted the veil of flesh and passed silently into the Great Beyond.

Now came crowds pouring into Bethany from all parts of the country. They paid their tribute at a funeral marked by austere simplicity. At the services the congregation sang a hymn commencing, "We've no continuing city here," Professor Charles Louis Loos offered a prayer, and Dr. Richardson delivered the sermon.[6] Toward the middle of the funeral oration, he said:

> And now he sleeps. No more shall we behold that intelligent countenance, beaming with a smile of kindly recognition. No more shall we hear that beloved voice in courteous greeting, or in lofty discourse upon themes of eternal interest. No more shall we clasp his friendly hand in love and fellowship. No more shall we see that commanding and venerable form. He sleeps.[7]

Richardson was conscious of speaking at the funeral of a great man as he said: "His public character is known to the wide world. His name is known—his influence has been felt in the most distant lands in which our vernacular is spoken." The giant oak in whose shadow Robert Richardson had lived for thirty-five years was fallen, and the empty sky was lonesome.

Robert Richardson went on to complete his contract at the college, teaching in the sessions and serving on the committees through the remainder of that term and still another; he also engaged to lecture for two months in 1867 in Bethany's new free course for ministers in the Biblical Institute. But he had now one passion, which cast his teaching into the shadow. That was to write the life of Alexander Campbell.

Thirty years earlier, in the "confidence and unreserve of friendship," he had told Alexander Campbell his secret ambition to write the story of his life; Campbell had been pleased, and had given his consent.[8]

The month of March, 1866, was not spent until the second Mrs. Alexander Campbell and four of her children made their formal request that Dr. Richardson should undertake such a biography:[9]

BETHANY, March 30, 1866.

DR. R. RICHARDSON:

Dear Brother in Christ:

A number of communications have been addressed to me on the subject of the memoirs of my lamented husband, conveying an earnest desire for their early appearance.

Desiring, on my own part, as well as that of my family, that this trust should be confided to one held in warm Christian sympathy and high personal esteem, such as I feel assured he ever felt for you during many years of intimate acquaintance and fellowship, the confident hope is entertained that you will comply with our heart-wishes in this respect. . . .

I remain, dear brother, your sister in the blessed hope of eternal life,

Selina H. Campbell.

In the above request the undersigned earnestly concur.

A. Campbell, Junior,
Virginia C. Thompson,
Decima C. Barclay,
W. P. Campbell.

The April issue of the *Millennial Harbinger* carried Richardson's announcement of his intention to write the life of Campbell and his request for letters and other biographical sources: "In pursuance of a long-cherished purpose, and in accordance with the wishes of Brother Campbell's family as well as of many esteemed brethren and friends, I design to complete, the Lord willing, as soon as practicable, a memoir of this eminent servant of God."[10]

From his study at Bethphage the doctor began at once to issue an enormous correspondence to his friends all over the nation whose letters and diaries might help him. Into his hands came bundles of papers from Mrs. Campbell, and there were almost countless volumes of magazines, thirty-six of the *Millennial Harbinger* alone, to be consulted.

Richardson was now exactly sixty years old and in good health, except for his eyes. These, weakened by his long aggravation of "amaurosis," were totally unequal to the task. Being unable to see for himself, he pressed the members of his family into service to read and write for him. His daughter Emma was nominated "amanuensis," and her father later remarked that her "patient services as reader and amanuensis" had "robbed her girlhood of many sportive hours."[11]

In addition to work in his study, Richardson, while still riding to and from Bethany to meet his classes, made jottings in his notebook, outlining chapters, recording remembered incidents, making assessments of character. Many of these were later thought too intimate to be admitted to the volume. Here, for instance, is a candid view of Alexander Campbell's driving purpose:

> First in importance in the estimation of Alexander Campbell was the Reformation, the cause of Primitive Christianity. For this he was ready to sacrifice his family, fortune, and even life. To this he had devoted all. For this he left home and at this he labored always. Next, were the spiritual and temporal interest of his own family. Next, his property—to care for it—to augment it in subordination to the two first points. Next, regard for personal friends—would not sacrifice property for them, but would aid them whenever it could be done with security to property—lend on interest—with security, and uneasy if not secured. Displeased if in any case a loser and apt to remember and dwell upon the loss. Next—welfare of the country of which he was a citizen.[12]

Another intimate insight, not for the book: "Mrs. C's excessive and absurd watch over his personal movements. Its effect in weakening his memory of places etc. Fully proved that he did and could transact business up to summer of 1855."

Another entry commented upon the general practice among all Bethany people of calling Campbell "the Bishop":

> A. C. regarded as Bishop of Wellsburg and Bethany. . . . An inquiry being started, and A. C. expostulated with, he said it was not with his concurrence or wish and that in fact he could not discharge the duties of Bishop in either church. He therefore in the M. H. disavowed the wish of being so regarded or addressed. . . . There being several persons at Bethany of the name Campbell, the people have come to style A. C. "the bishop," partly by way of distinction—but partly in sport (at least at first). It has now come to be his common designation. . . . The students carry this abroad so that it is gradually becoming his designation everywhere.

As a literary man, Richardson entered a note on Campbell's style: "His first efforts somewhat stiff . . . but the style here modified by the assumption of character—but the structure of sentences and use of words excellent and according to good English usage. He was always opposed to barbarism—preferred simple expressions. After the College was established fell into bad habit of using technical terms and high sounding words."

The writing of this biography required three years. Emma, later Mrs. G. L. Wharton, missionary to India, shows us the busy scene in the study:

> He went into it with a keen enjoyment and his interest never flagged during the three years which it took to complete the great work. He would go up to his little study immediately after breakfast every morning and I with him. He would seat himself in the plain, straight chair he always occupied, and I at the

desk, when the work of dictation and inscribing began, to be continued uninterruptedly, except for the dinner hour, until three or four o'clock in the afternoon when he would say to me, "Now run away and play," and he would saddle his horse and ride away to Bethany for the Mail or on other business.

Emma, born September 2, 1852, was in her middle teens when these responsibilities began. She carried this position for the next ten years.

It was always a marvel to me with what facility he wrote or dictated. Just as fast as I could write, the words came from his mouth, and there was seldom a correction or rewriting of a word or sentence, or hesitation of any kind, though occasionally he would have me stop and consult the Dictionary for a word of which he was not quite certain. However, this was seldom. In this way, also, he dictated to me all his letters, the "Communings in the Sanctuary" and "Office of the Holy Spirit" besides his numerous articles for periodicals.[13]

Finally, when the first draft of the manuscript for Volume I was completed in December, 1867,[14] Mr. William Uhlrich copied the whole of it and prepared it for the printers. Of this experience he later wrote:

I would like to see the old Dr. Richardson place up on the hill, about two miles out. I spent about six weeks at his place when he was writing the life of Alexander Campbell. His eyes were poor and most of it was written by his daughter at his dictation, on all kinds of paper and on both sides. I had to re-write all of it on one side of the page and leave a margin for notes. This was all done with pen and ink, mostly quill pen. Then I had to read it all over to the doctor from beginning to end to see that the spelling and punctuation were correct. It was quite an experience for me.[15]

The book was brought out by J. B. Lippincott and Company, Philadelphia. Written in a clear, Addisonian prose, well printed and nicely bound, these two volumes totaled nearly 1,300 pages and made a most impressive work.

The first volume appeared in the summer of 1868. Isaac Errett, having just completed a review of it for his new magazine, the *Christian Standard,* wrote his friend from Cleveland on June 22, 1868:

> I have just finished a review of your Memoirs for next week's paper. Allow me to congratulate you on your success in producing a much needed volume, which will go far to correct wrong tendencies, and to call us back to the *first principles* of this movement. It is admirably and faithfully done. . . . I pray for you that you may be *just* and faithful in your second volume. Mr. C. had nothing to fear in your hands; but where he was wrong, and his errors, injurious, as in the matter of hireling preachers, let it come out. I hope too, that his constant sympathy with Protestantism and his infinite superiority to our close-communion advocates, in his recognition of the piety and spiritual worth of Pedobaptists, will, in a quiet way, be made to appear. Pardon these suggestions. I only meant to congratulate you and thank you for your elegant volume.[16]

When the second volume came out, near the close of 1869, Isaac Errett voiced the nearly universal pleasure in the completed work, to which Richardson replied:

> BETHPHAGE, Dec. 24, 1869.
>
> DEAR BRO. ERRETT:
>
> I have just received your very kind letter of 18th inst. and am happy to find that you are pleased with the 2nd vol. of Bro. C's Memoirs. . . .

I have thought, with you, that some dissatisfaction might arise in regard to the brief notices given of Bro. C's co-laborers. . . . As to Fanning, I would have omitted his name entirely from the volume, only that he was Bro. C's traveling companion on 2 occasions, and I thought such an omission might lead some to think I cherished animosity against the poor man for his former slanderous abuse of me. It was in mercy to him that I . . . simply stated *all* that was to his credit. . . .

The name of B. F. [Benjamin Franklin] does not occur in the volume because there was no link connecting him with Bro. C.— no private letters—no notice in the Harbinger—no cooperation in personal labors. . . . Want of space forbade me to do more. As it was I had to leave out nearly 200 pages of interesting matter and with all my condensing, make the book much larger than the first at great expense. . . .

The two-volume work sold at $3.50, with a 40-cent charge for postage.[17] In 1871 a new edition, presenting the two volumes in one cover, was brought out. Richardson's arrangements with the publishers were not those of a shrewd businessman. He was left to bear the expense of publication himself. The Campbell heirs did not offer to help. The sale of the book did not match the cost, and the doctor was never able to clear himself of the debt which this service to the Disciples incurred. Constituted as he was, this last debt weighed heavily upon him during his declining years.

While Dr. Richardson was writing the *Memoirs,* he was also the recipient of numerous demands from many parts of the nation. On July 21, 1868, he received an appeal from J. Hartzel, of Davenport, Iowa, asking him to use his pen against a trend toward abuse of authority by elders in local congregations. Then on March 27, 1869, Robert Graham solicited articles for the *Apostolic Times;* and the same year, Isaac Errett wanted Robert Richardson's assistance as contributing editor to the *Christian Standard.*

Acceding to these requests, the doctor sat in his Bethphage study, pouring forth words to strengthen and sustain the cause whose chief advocate now slept beneath the pines of the Campbell cemetery on the hill opposite the mansion.

Chapter XVII

HOME TO BETHPHAGE

Robert Richardson's college teaching days were over. As the decade turned into the 1870's, he was back in his initial role, having again resumed his post on the Board of Trustees in July, 1869.[1] During the next six years he never missed a meeting of this body. Helping plan curriculum, moving to create the degrees of Bachelor of Science and Master of Science, serving on the Executive Committee, signing diplomas, securing faculty members, sitting through long discussions on tangled finances, he worked with James A. Garfield and other trustees in steering the college through the postwar storm. In the September meeting, 1870, plans were made for the completion of Commencement Hall, originally planned to be the left wing of the college structure. This new building was dedicated on June 13, 1872, making Bethany's collegiate Gothic crown complete. Richardson shared in the ceremonies.[2]

With some apprehension he watched the college deficit climb, within five years, from $6,500 to $17,000. These deficits were paid out of the endowment. He saw the endowment melt away to pay salaries and meet building costs until it promised to disappear altogether by the end of the decade. Strong members of the faculty were resigning, and President Pendleton himself was thinking of taking a state political office.[3] The future of his beloved Bethany was precarious and becoming more so.

225

Willie, the baby of the family, had now grown to manhood and had entered the college in his father's sixty-sixth year. When he graduated in 1876, it was to enter the legal profession. Of the other sons, Nathaniel also had been a lawyer, rising to distinction in Wheeling. He had even served a term in the Virginia state legislature. Tragically he had perished in the flames of a Wellsburg hotel fire on March 14, 1873, the second and last bereavement Robert Richardson was to suffer from among his ten children.[4] Edgar was serving out his apprenticeship as a pharmacist in Pittsburgh, and John was preparing to take over the farm. Of the girls, Anne and Mary were married, but Fannie, Julia, and Emma were still at home. Of these, only Julia was to remain unmarried. Even so, the others stayed close under the family rooftree and did not marry until after his death. It was a close-knit family, dwelling in a rambling old house that had seen much living.

Now came the grandchildren to visit and enliven the old house with their laughter. Grandfather Richardson, presiding over the dinner table with his grace before and after meals and his strict control of the conversation, seemed to them austere and almost frightening. How could they know that their presence delighted him so much that he could not utter his joy?

In the music room the grown children and their guests gathered around the piano as of old to sing and to play their favorite numbers. At the family-worship circle, Father Richardson led them, as he had done for years, in the singing of his best loved hymns: "God moves in a mysterious way," "From all that dwell below the skies," and "Jesus, and shall it ever be." The paintings on the wall, painted by Robert himself and by Mary and Julia, carried Richardson's mind back to his boyhood days under his gentle, artistic mother at 58 Fourth Street.

Sometimes the mood of reminiscence came upon this happy family as they remembered, amid laughter, some of the incidents which brightened their childhood. There had been that time when Father felt that Julia's delicate condition would improve with a sea voyage. So he had taken her to New York and boarded ship for Portland, Maine, engaging a nurse to look after Julia when she should become seasick. When they were at sea, both the nurse and Dr. Richardson had become miserably seasick, but Julia remained calmly unaffected! Her father said that she was the most perverse young lady he ever knew.

Or they recalled the times Father had undertaken to cure drunkards, bringing them under the family roof and nursing them for months. Once, for as long as four years, he took in and cared for an old man who had sunk to the lowest depths through drink. This alcoholic ate at the family table with them and sat as one of the family at the fireside. As long as he was within that charmed circle, he was safe from his demon; but once he was outside, it pounced upon him. Again and again he returned to his haven, and every time he was taken in under the sheltering roof without reproach.

They remembered with what confidence they had endured every childhood sickness, perfectly sure that their father, whom they thought the wisest physician in the world, could make them well again.

The time they had eaten Thanksgiving dinner at the home of Professor Ross came to mind. That short little professor had stood up to carve the turkey, and someone had pulled back his chair to give him room. With the carving completed, and with a hand on the fork which was anchored firmly in the turkey, the little professor had sat down to find the chair wasn't there. The turkey was flipped into the air, and soon joined the professor and his dignity on the floor!

Demands upon Richardson in these years increased rather than diminished. In 1872 he gathered together some of his previous essays to use as the content of a book bearing the title, *The Office of the Holy Spirit*. Nearly every Disciple magazine asked for his articles. Personal correspondence poured in upon him. Emma, schooled by years as his private secretary, read to him and wrote for him. Often, after she had read a letter, and her father had indicated the general nature of his answer, she composed the reply; except for a word here or there, he approved and signed it unchanged.

He worked and wrote to support the cause of cooperation and enlightenment in the brotherhood. On February 3, 1873, he wrote an extremely long letter of some 3,000 words to a Mr. Magarey in Australia, one paragraph of which was as follows:

> I entirely agree with you as to the narrowness of our English brethren on the communion question & in regard to missionary work. The cause can never prosper in Great Britain until they outgrow their errors in these subjects. The brethren here have

not recovered from the wrong views they formerly entertained respecting missions, and it is with the greatest difficulty they can be induced to contribute.

He favored printed lesson helps for Sunday school, use of instrumental music in churches, and missionary societies. He even contemplated a published book of family prayers. In the letter from which the preceding paragraph is quoted, he said:

The important subject of family prayer . . . is one which has been often before me, and often discussed with Bro. A. Campbell, his revered father, W. Scott & others in years that are past to return no more. The aid of a book of devotion with forms of prayer etc., was then and has been since occasionally suggested. A few weeks ago, Bro. J. S. Lamar had an article in the *Christian Standard* strongly recommending such a work. His proposition, however has not been well received. I do not myself see any absolute impropriety in the use of such a Formula. . . . There is no doubt that the regular extemporaneous family prayers & thanksgivings at table constantly tend to assume a fixed form of expression among all religious people, and, for that matter, might as well be printed and read, as constantly repeated from memory. I have no doubt that suitable forms of devotion would greatly aid timid persons, and might induce them to bring their families together for the worship of God. There would certainly be no impropriety in preparing such a Manual.[5]

When he addressed the American Christian Missionary Society in 1870, he deplored "that sort of church independency which leads a dozen or two to assemble and style themselves '*the* Church of Christ,' and, while doing nothing beyond self-edification, glory in the thought that they are '*the* pillar and support of the truth.'" "What truth do they support?" he asked. "The world does not even know of their existence, and they live and die without one earnest forth-putting of missionary enterprise to make the world better."[6]

He spent many moments of these years worrying over debt. Robert Richardson's publishing ventures never brought him any financial profit. His debt from them was cleared years later only after his daughter Fannie took matters in hand and, having sold the books in stock and having gathered funds from her brothers and sisters, finally discharged the obligation. To quote again from Richardson's letter to Magarey:

> In regards to the Messrs. Lippincott. I hardly know what to make of them. They are certainly shamefully remiss as to their correspondence, and business obligations. I wrote to them that you had forwarded a draft. . . . Two years ago they sent me a brief abstract of ac. making it appear that I was indebted to them upwards of $1500. I wrote to them stating that this was much more than I expected, and that I desired to have the account in detail so that I could understand the matter. In the meantime I sent them $1,000.—but from that day to this, I have been unable to get from them a copy of my account on their books, or any account at all of sales of books. . . . I am sorry now that I ever undertook the publication of the book [*Memoirs of Alexander Campbell*] myself, as it has proved to be a troublesome & losing business.

From the beginning of 1872, Richardson began to suffer from violent paroxysms about the heart. As a physician he was able quickly to diagnose his own condition. It was angina pectoris. Though he tried digitalis and other remedies, he knew that he carried his death sentence within him. If he walked twenty-five or thirty yards, the peculiar distress began, increasing in intensity with every step, until he was compelled to stop and remain quiet for several minutes. While he remained quietly in his study or rode gently on horseback, he suffered little. But he was always conscious of a feeling that the disease was ever present and, like a tiger in a jungle, ready at any time to spring.

Robert's brother Edward, also a physician, had been in the habit of paying an annual visit to Bethphage. He had a successful practice in Louisville, Kentucky. These two brothers, the eldest and youngest of a family of eleven, were singularly fond of each other. Dr. Edward felt that he owed much to Dr. Robert, and he looked upon him almost as a father. They were very congenial, and the two of them greatly enjoyed these annual visits. In earlier years, they took long walks over the farm and spent the days in expansive conversation. After the heart attacks, Edward continued to come, and, except that the walks were now shorter, they walked and talked as usual; but the physician's eye of the younger brother could read the future, and a cloud somewhat shadowed the formerly sunny hours of his visit.

Among the topics on which the brothers dwelt this year was the advances which had been made in their own science. Antisepsis and anesthesia had come. Blistering and bleeding had gone. The "heroic" medicine of violent drugs had been discontinued, and with it the dogmatism of the schools. Medicine had become teachable. It was going to school to the facts, and it was coming of age.

Robert Richardson was too competent a physician himself not to know that his days were numbered. One day in 1875 he took John aside, told him of his approaching attack, and outlined the farm work for a year in advance. Together they planned the care of the stock, the fruit, and the crops for the next twelve months.[7]

Then in February of 1876 it came. Having spent the morning of February 18 in his study, he came down to dinner in an unusually happy mood. He ate heartily, keeping up a lively conversation. John, Emma, and his wife, Rebekah, were the only ones at home. When dinner was over, he left the room and went out into the yard for a short stroll. A few moments later, John followed, only to find him prostrate and unconscious on the ground.

John gathered him up into his arms and carried him into the house and laid him on the bed. Then he rode off to Bethany as fast as he could to bring Dr. Whittsett. Dr. Hukill, of West Liberty, was also called. After a brief time Richardson regained consciousness, and in the course of a week he was in his accustomed place in the family circle, but he had lost the power of speech, and the physicians offered no hope of recovery.

His speechlessness was not a paralysis of the vocal organs but of the nerve centers controlling the formation of words and sentences. Neither was he able to write. Several times he sat down at his desk and tried to write, but he was unable to do so. In a strange series of scratches he once tried to copy the fourteenth chapter of John, but after working painfully for a long time and making poor progress, he laid the pen aside and sadly pushed the paper from him.

His mind remained clear, however. His eyes were no weaker than formerly, and he was able to read some of his heavy mail and the newspapers. Emma still did most of his reading for him. Sometimes he came to her with a letter to which he wished her to reply, but instead of writing at his dictation, she wrote what she thought he would wish to say, and then read it aloud for his approval. By nodding and shaking his head, he was able to make her understand his corrections, and she wrote and revised until she had the letter as he wished it.

Months passed. He seemed calm and untroubled. He sat long hours in his accustomed chair at the fireside, with a look of perfect rest and peace on his face. He took short walks about the farm and showed an interest in all that was going on. Often he went with John to inspect and approve of what was being done.

In September, his brother Edward came for his annual visit. They walked as usual and sat together, but one voice that had always joined in the animated conversation was mute. It was a sad visit for Edward, but on his brother's brow there was no cloud. Instead, there was peace and love and a calm, expectant serenity. He never seemed happier.

Attended faithfully by his two physicians, he refused once to take the medicine prescribed by one of them. He also refused for several meals to eat or drink, until Rebekah discovered that he had the idea that she was putting this medicine into his food and drink. Later, a specialist gave the opinion that this particular medicine would have been fatal. Only once did he prescribe for himself. Then he tried to tell the attending doctor the name of the medicine he wanted. Finally, he tried to write it and, after much effort, at length succeeded in making the word legible. When the other physician saw the recommended treatment, he admitted it to be better than the one he had himself prescribed.

One day Willie was sent off to Bethany on an errand. As was the custom at Bethphage, he rode a horse. He had been gone only a little while when it was noticed by other members of the family that Dr. Richardson was much disturbed. After asking him numerous questions, to which he could nod or shake his head in a process of elimination, Emma finally learned that he was disturbed by something about Willie. After questioning him further, she understood him to want to know whether or not Willie had put the blanket under the saddle when he started for the village. When Emma assured him that Willie had done so, he had no further uneasiness.

Former students and associates often called on him in these months of silence. He was avid for their stories of what was happening in the college and in the brotherhood. With nods and signs he encouraged them to talk and by the benediction of his own peace he smoothed away their awkwardness and embarrassment.

The year 1876 came around to October, and the leaves on the hills became a fairyland of color. Robert Richardson had been imprisoned in silence for eight months. Sunday, October 22, dawned fair and with the warmth of Indian summer. In the forenoon some of the family drove to the Bethany church. About three o'clock in the afternoon, Richardson started for a walk over the farm, accompanied by Emma. He seemed unusually quiet and meditative as he walked slowly, and with head slightly bowed, up to the top of the hill overlooking Bethany.

He had always loved that view, and he stood for a long time looking at it. He saw the valley of the Buffalo, from below "the narrows" to beyond the Campbell home. In one arm of the creek's winding "S" nestled the village of Bethany, and in the other the mansion, study, and cemetery of the Campbells. On the hill above the village stood the college buildings, in new Gothic splendor. Just below him lay the patchwork quilt of cultivated fields in the bottom-land of "Logan's Hollow." He surveyed it all, with welling memories and thoughts locked up in a prison of silence. He looked over to the place where Alexander Campbell slept and where he, too, would rest and then turned slowly away.

Now, his gaze fell upon the amphitheatre of Bethphage, clothed in her autumn colors. These, to him, were acres of Paradise. The rambling house, grown with the family to nineteen rooms, nestled securely on the stage amid its gardens with shrubs, vines, and trees. Around it there fanned out the fields, divided by osage orange hedges. Here were his orchards, his gardens, his fields; and there his home and hearth. He looked long and lovingly upon this scene—Bethphage, "nigh unto Bethany."

Slowly he and Emma walked down the hill and through the orchard to the house. He sat alone on the porch. Shortly a violent storm with lightning and thunder came up. It lasted for about half an hour. Afterward there was calm. At dark, as was his custom since the beginning of his illness, Richardson passed through the living room on his way to bed. To Rebekah and Emma, who were sitting there, he motioned good night, but as he neared Rebekah's chair he stopped and passed both hands over her hair affectionately, murmured an inarticulate "good night" and went on into his bedroom. A few minutes afterward, Emma heard the sound of labored breathing. When she reached him, his heart was still!

The End

NOTES

CHAPTER I

1. For this letter and Robert Richardson's reply, see *Christian Baptist*, 14th ed., pp. 599ff.

2. Matt. 10:34-37, Campbell's version, *Living Oracles*, 1826.

3. Goodnight's transcript of Richardson's private papers.

CHAPTER II

1. Trinity Cathedral records.

2. Agnes Lynch Starrett, *Through One Hundred and Fifty Years*, p. 164. University of Pittsburgh Press.

3. Robert Richardson, *Memoirs of Alexander Campbell*, Vol. I, p. 463.

4. *Idem*, p. 464.

5. *Idem*, p. 506.

6. *Idem*, p. 509.

7. Dwight E. Stevenson, *Walter Scott: Voice of the Golden Oracle*, pp. 30-32. Christian Board of Publication, St. Louis, 1946.

8. *Idem*, pp. 36f.

9. Richardson, *op. cit.* Vol. I, p. 508.

CHAPTER III

1. Stevenson, *Walter Scott: Voice of the Golden Oracle*, p. 41.

2. Starrett, *Through One Hundred and Fifty Years*, pp. 75f.

3. Leland D. Baldwin, *Pittsburgh, the Story of a City*, pp. 157f.

4. *Idem*, pp. 250f.

5. Theodore Diller, *Pioneer Medicine in Western Pennsylvania*, pp. 42f. Paul B. Hoeber, Inc., Medical Book Department of Harper & Brothers, New York and London.

6. Official records of the Medical School, confirmed by a letter from the assistant dean, April 7, 1947.

7. *Christian Baptist*, 14th ed., p. 601.

8. Richardson, *Memoirs of Alexander Campbell*, Vol. II, p. 297.

9. Stevenson, *op. cit.* pp. 71-80.

10. Winfred E. Garrison, *Religion Follows the Frontier*, p. 200. Harper & Brothers, New York and London, 1931.

11. Richardson, *op. cit.* Vol. II, p. 298.

CHAPTER IV

1. Richardson, *Memoirs of Alexander Campbell*, Vol. II, p. 299.

2. M. C. Tiers, *The Christian Portrait Gallery*, p. 158.

3. W. C. Morro, *Brother McGarvey*, p. 158. Bethany Press, St. Louis, 1940.

4. *Millennial Harbinger*, 1830, p. 1.

5. Richardson, *op. cit.*, pp. 326f.

6. *Millennial Harbinger*, 1830, p. 206.

7. *Evangelist*, 1832, p. 203.

8. *Idem*, p. 205.

9. *Idem,* pp. 211f.

10. Wellsburg church records, written in Robert Richardson's hand.

CHAPTER V

1. *Evangelist,* 1834, pp. 34f., 49f., 110f.

2. *Idem,* pp. 25-29, 98-109.

3. Richardson, *Memoirs of Alexander Campbell,* Vol. II, pp. 394f. See also, *Evangelist,* 1834, pp. 97f., 121f.

4. *Millennial Harbinger,* 1834, pp. 385-444.

5. Carthage church records.

6. Date of birth on tombstone, Campbell Cemetery, Bethany.

7. Goodnight's transcript of Richardson's private papers; a letter by Alexander Campbell to Robert Richardson, Dec. 29, 1835.

8. *Millennial Harbinger,* 1835, p. 612, dated Nov. 3, 1835.

9. *Idem,* pp. 617f.

10. *Idem,* 1836, p. 184.

11. W. T. Moore, *Comprehensive History of the Disciples of Christ,* p. 281. Fleming H. Revell Co., New York, London, Edinburgh, 1909.

CHAPTER VI

1. *Millennial Harbinger,* 1836, p. 239.

2. *Idem,* 1835, p. 618.

3. *Idem,* 1836, p. 233.

4. *Idem,* pp. 393f.

5. *Idem,* pp. 333, 335.

6. *Idem,* 1838, p. 199.

7. Goodnight's transcript of Richardson's private papers.

8. *Millennial Harbinger,* 1836, pp. 345-49.

9. B. L. Smith, *Alexander Campbell,* p. 325. Bethany Press, St. Louis, 1930.

10. Moore, *Comprehensive History of the Disciples of Christ,* p. 281.

11. *Millennial Harbinger,* 1836, p. 480.

12. *Idem,* 1837, pp. 451-60.

13. *Idem,* pp. 500-506.

14. *Idem,* 1838, p. 479.

CHAPTER VII

1. *Millennial Harbinger,* 1839, p. 289.

2. W. R. Warren, *The Life and Labors of Archibald McLean,* pp. 60f. United Christian Missionary Society, Indianapolis, 1923.

3. Sue Sublette, in the *Christian Standard,* Nov. 14, 1896.

4. *Millennial Harbinger,* 1839, pp. 446-51.

CHAPTER VIII

1. *Millennial Harbinger,* 1839, p. 448. Cf. W. K. Woolery, *Bethany Years,* pp. 28f.

2. *Millennial Harbinger,* 1839, p. 450.

3. Woolery, *op. cit.,* p. 31.

4. Charter of Bethany College, in *Millennial Harbinger,* 1840, pp. 176-79.

5. Minutes of the Board of Trustees of Bethany College.

6. *Millennial Harbinger,* 1840, pp. 509f.

7. *Idem,* p. 179.

8. *Idem,* 1841, p. 269.

9. Woolery, *op. cit.*, pp. 35f.

10. *Idem*, p. 54.

11. *Idem*, p. 48.

12. *Millennial Harbinger*, 1842, p. 36.

13. Minutes of the Board of Trustees of Bethany College.

14. *Millennial Harbinger*, 1842, pp. 29-33.

15. Woolery, *op. cit.*, p. 68.

16. Morro, *Brother McGarvey*, p. 56.

CHAPTER IX

1. Minutes of the Board of Trustees of Bethany College.

2. *Millennial Harbinger*, 1842, p. 319.

3. Minutes of the Board of Trustees of Bethany College.

4. *Millennial Harbinger*, 1842, p. 143.

5. *Idem*, p. 383.

6. *Idem*, 1843, p. 473.

7. Bethany College Catalogue, July, 1843.

8. *Millennial Harbinger*, 1843, pp. 281-83.

9. *Idem*, p. 373.

10. *Idem*, p. 277.

11. This whole section on the power of the president and the rights of the professors is based on the minutes of the Board of Trustees of Bethany College.

12. *Millennial Harbinger*, 1841, pp. 491f.

13. *Idem*, pp. 241-45.

14. *Idem*, 1843, pp. 124-28.

15. Smith, *Alexander Campbell*, p. 328.

16. Goodnight's transcript of Richardson's private papers; a letter from Bethphage, July 16, 1857.

17. *Millennial Harbinger*, 1843, p. 567.

18. *Idem*, 1854, pp. 181-200.

CHAPTER X

1. *Millennial Harbinger*, 1848, p. 530.

2. A. S. Hayden, *Early History of the Disciples in the Western Reserve, Ohio*, pp. 260-66. Chase & Hall, Cincinnati, 1875.

3. *Millennial Harbinger*, 1847, p. 716.

4. *Idem*, p. 134.

5. *Idem*, 1849, pp. 661-64.

CHAPTER XI

1. Frederick D. Power, *Life of William Kimbrough Pentleton*, p. 139. Christian Publishing Co., St. Louis, 1902.

2. Minutes of the Board of Trustees of Bethany College, July 3, 1851.

3. Woolery, *Bethany Years*, pp. 45f.

4. *Millennial Harbinger*, 1854, pp. 117f.

5. Wheeling *Daily Intelligencer*, June 21, 1855.

6. *Idem*, June 27, 1855.

7. Mary Richardson Chapline, "Father's Likes and Dislikes."

8. *Millennial Harbinger*, 1854, p. 653.

9. *Idem*, 1855, p. 293.

10. *Idem*, pp. 517-20.

11. *Idem*, 1853, p. 297.

12. *Idem*, p. 117.

13. *Idem*, 1854, p. 232.

14. Robert Richardson, *Principles and Objects of the Religious Reformation*, pp. 6f.

15. *Idem*, p. 7.

16. *Idem*, p. 13.

17. *Idem*, p. 26.

18. *Idem*, pp. 26f.

19. *Idem*, p. 29.

20. *Idem*, p. 31.

21. *Idem*, p. 37.

22. *Idem*, p. 44.

23. J. S. Lamar, *Memoirs of Isaac Errett*, Vol. I, p. 147. Standard Publishing Co., Cincinnati, 1893.

CHAPTER XII

1. *Millennial Harbinger*, 1856, p. 151.

2. *Idem*, p. 174.

3. W. K. Pendleton's letters.

4. *Millennial Harbinger*, 1856, p. 154.

5. *Idem*, 1857, pp. 82-85.

6. Goodnight's transcript of Richardson's private papers.

7. Robert Richardson, *Communings in the Sanctuary*, pp. 32f. Transylvania Press (year of publication unknown).

8. Morro, *Brother McGarvey*, p. 60.

9. Richardson, *op. cit.*, p. 18.

10. *Idem*, pp. 68f.

11. *Idem*, pp. 143f.

12. *Idem,* pp. 112f.

13. *Idem*, p. 73.

14. *Idem*, pp. 114f.

15. *Idem*, p. 156.

16. *Idem,* p. 147.

17. *Idem*, pp. 71f.

CHAPTER XIII

1. *Millennial Harbinger*, 1857, p. 407.

2. Woolery, *Bethany Years*, p. 60.

3. *Millennial Harbinger*, 1857, p. 134.

4. The details of the controversies traced in this chapter are to be found in the following pages of the *Millennial Harbinger*: 1857, pp. 134-37, 191-97, 255-59, 265-76, 328-36, 395-406, 433-48, 481-85, 491-95, 546-51, 559-67, 573-80, 692-703; 1858, pp. 86, 199-205, 289f., 353; 1859, pp. 39f., 54; also in the *Evangelist* for 1858, pp. 67f.; also in the private correspondence of Robert Richardson with Philip S. Fall for July 30, 1857, Aug. 24, 1857, Sept. 23, 1857, Dec. 15, 1858, Dec. 19, 1859; with Isaac Errett for July 16, 1857; and with Reuben L. Coleman for July 16, 1857; also in Alexander Campbell's letter to P. S. Fall for Jan. 4, 1860; and the minutes of the Board of Trustees of Bethany College. The letters, except for those to P. S. Fall, are in Goodnight's transcript of Richardson's private papers.

5. Woolery, *op. cit.*, p. 89.

6. Minutes of the Board of Trustees of Bethany College.

CHAPTER XIV

1. Richardson to P. S. Fall, Dec. 15, 1858.

2. *Ibid.*

3. This and succeeding items of information about Bacon College and Kentucky University, except where noted, are from Alonzo W. Fortune, *The Disciples in Kentucky*, pp. 191-94.

4. Minutes of the Board of Curators, Kentucky University.

5. Goodnight's transcript of Richardson's private papers.

6. Minutes of the Board of Curators, Kentucky University.

7. Goodnight's transcript of Richardson's private papers.

8. Philip S. Fall correspondence.

9. *Millennial Harbinger*, 1859, pp. 39f., 54.

10. Minutes of the Board of Trustees of Bethany College.

11. Woolery, *Bethany Years*, pp. 90-92.

12. Minutes of the Board of Trustees of Bethany College.

13. *Biographical and Historical Catalogue of Washington and Jefferson College*, p. 563. George H. Buchanan Co., Philadelphia, 1902.

14. *Millennial Harbinger*, 1859, p. 532.

15. *Idem*, p. 597.

CHAPTER XV

1. Fortune, *The Disciples in Kentucky*, p. 194.

2. Catalogue of Kentucky University, 1861, p. 20.

3. Fortune, *op. cit.*, p. 194.

4. *Millennial Harbinger*, 1860, p. 474.

5. Alexander Campbell to P. S. Fall, Jan. 4, 1860.

6. Richardson to P. S. Fall, Dec. 19, 1859.

7. *Millennial Harbinger*, 1862, pp. 41f.

8. *Idem*, 1861, pp. 712f.

9. *Idem*, 1862, pp. 97f. (footnote).

10. *Idem*, 1861, p. 711.

11. *Idem*, pp. 712f.

12. Robert Milligan letter to Richardson, Aug. 11, 1862, in Goodnight's transcript of Richardson's private papers.

13. Fortune, *op. cit.*, pp. 194f.

14. *Millennial Harbinger*, 1867, pp. 277-85.

15. P. S. Fall to Richardson, Dec. 13, 1862.

16. Oral tradition, through Mrs. W. W. Pilchard, Bethany.

17. Fortune, *op. cit.*, pp. 194f.

CHAPTER XVI

1. *Catalogue of the Officers, Alumni and Students of Bethany College for the 20th, 21st, 22nd, 23rd, and 24th Sessions, Ending July 4, 1865*, p. 14.

2. *Millennial Harbinger*, 1865, pp. 429f.

3. Richardson, *Memoirs of Alexander Campbell*, Vol. II, p. 674.

4. *Idem*, pp. 674f.

5. *Millennial Harbinger*, 1866, p. 141.

6. Richardson, *op. cit.*, p. 679.

7. *Millennial Harbinger*, 1866, pp. 141f.

8. Richardson, *op. cit.*, Vol. I, p. 2.

9. *Idem*, p. 3.

10. *Millennial Harbinger*, 1866, p. 185.

11. Richardson, *op. cit.*, p. 3.

12. Robert Richardson notebook.

13. Mrs. G. L. Wharton, "Father's Last Days."

14. Richardson, *op. cit.*, p. 5.

15. Goodnight's transcript of Richardson's private papers.

16. Isaac Errett to Richardson, June 22, 1868, in Goodnight's transcript of Richardson's private papers.

17. *Millennial Harbinger*, 1869, p. 718.

CHAPTER XVII

1. *Millennial Harbinger*, 1869, p. 405.

2. Minutes of the Board of Trustees of Bethany College.

3. Woolery, *Bethany Years*, p. 117.

4. Bethany oral tradition.

5. Goodnight's transcript of Richardson's private papers.

6. Lamar, *Memoirs of Isaac Errett*, Vol. II, p. 44.

7. Wharton, "Father's Last Days."

BIBLIOGRAPHY

I. GENERAL BACKGROUND HISTORY

Adams, James Truslow. *The Epic of America*. Little, Brown & Co., Boston, 1935.

Ambler, Charles Henry. *West Virginia Stories and Biographies*. Rand McNally & Co., 1937.

Baldwin, Leland D. *Pittsburgh, the Story of a City*. University of Pittsburgh Press, 1938.

Boyd, Peter. *History of Northern West Virginia Panhandle*. Historical Publishing Co., Topeka and Indianapolis, 1927.

Diller, Theodore. *Pioneer Medicine in Western Pennsylvania*. Paul B. Hoeber, Inc., New York, 1927.

Flexner, James Thomas. *Doctors on Horseback, Pioneers of American Medicine*. Garden City Publishing Co., 1939.

Hoffman, Sylvan; and Grattan, C. Hartley (ed.). *News of the Nation, A Newspaper History of the United States*. Garden City Publishing Co., 1943.

Jacob, J. G. *Brooke County Record of Prominent Events*. Wellsburg Herald, 1882.

Starrett, Agnes Lynch. *Through One Hundred and Fifty Years, The University of Pittsburgh*. University of Pittsburgh Press, 1937.

II. GENERAL DISCIPLE HISTORY

Fortune, Alonzo Willard. *The Disciples in Kentucky*. Convention of Christian Churches in Kentucky, 1932.

Garrison, Winfred Ernest. *An American Religious Movement*. Bethany Press, St. Louis, 1945.

————. *Religion Follows the Frontier*. Harper & Brothers, New York, 1931.

Hayden, A. S. *Early History of the Disciples in the Western Reserve, Ohio*. Chase & Hall, Cincinnati, 1875.

Moore, W. T. *A Comprehensive History of the Disciples of Christ*. Fleming H. Revell Co., New York, London, and Edinburgh, 1909.

Rogers, James R. *The Cane Ridge Meeting-house*. Standard Publishing Co., Cincinnati, 1910.

Spencer, Claude E. *Periodicals of the Disciples of Christ*. Disciples of Christ Historical Society, Canton, Mo., 1943.

————. *An Author Catalog of Disciples of Christ.* Disciples of Christ Historical Society, 1946.

Woolery, William K. *Bethany Years.* Standard Printing and Publishing Co., Huntington, W. Va., 1941.

III. *CHAPTERS OR PORTIONS OF BOOKS DEALING CHIEFLY WITH THE LIFE OF ROBERT RICHARDSON*

Garrison, Winfred Ernest. Article, "Robert Richardson," in the *Dictionary of American Biography,* Vol. 15, 1935.

Smith, Benjamin Lyon. *Alexander Campbell,* Chapter 21, "Robert Richardson," Bethany Press, St. Louis, 1930.

Sublette, Sue. "A Visit to Bethany," in the *Christian Standard,* Nov. 14, 1896.

Tiers, M. C. *The Christian Portrait Gallery.* Franklin Type Foundry, Cincinnati, 1864.

IV. *BIOGRAPHIES OF ALLIED LEADERS*

Baxter, William. *Life of Elder Walter Scott.* Bosworth, Chase & Hall, Cincinnati, 1874.

Hanna, William Herbert. *Thomas Campbell, Seceder and Christian Union Advocate.* Standard Publishing Co., Cincinnati, 1935.

Lamar, J. S. *Memoirs of Isaac Errett, with Selections from His Writings* (2 vol.). Standard Publishing Co., 1893.

Morro, William Charles. *Brother McGarvey.* Bethany Press, St. Louis, 1940.

Power, Frederick D. *Life of William Kimbrough Pendleton.* Christian Publishing Co., St. Louis, 1902.

Smith, Benjamin Lyon. *Alexander Campbell.* Bethany Press, 1930.

Stevenson, Dwight E. *Walter Scott: Voice of the Golden Oracle.* Christian Board of Publication, St. Louis, 1946.

Warren, William Robinson. *The Life and Labors of Archibald McLean.* United Christian Missionary Society, Indianapolis, 1923.

V. *BOOKS WRITTEN BY ROBERT RICHARDSON*

A Scriptural View of the Office of the Holy Spirit. Bosworth, Chase & Hall, Cincinnati, 1872.

Communings in the Sanctuary. Transylvania Printing and Publishing Co., Lexington (year of publication unknown).

Memoirs of Alexander Campbell: Embracing a View of the Origin, Progress and Principles of the Religious Reformation Which He Advocated (2 vol.). J. B. Lippincott & Co., Philadelphia, 1868, 1870.

BIBLIOGRAPHY

The Principles and Objects of the Religious Reformation Urged by A. Campbell and Others, Briefly Stated and Explained. Printed and published by A. Campbell, Bethany, 1853.

VI. *OTHER WORKS CONTAINING RICHARDSON'S WRITINGS*

Bates, Daniel (ed.). *Evangelist.* Mount Pleasant, Fort Madison, Davenport, Iowa, 1850-64.

Campbell, Alexander (ed.). *Christian Baptist.* Buffaloe and Bethany, Va., 1823-30.

Campbell, Alexander (ed.). *Introductory Addresses, Delivered at the Organization of Bethany College, November 2nd, 1841,* "General Introductory Discourse." A. Campbell, publisher, Bethany, Va., 1841.

Campbell, Alexander, *et al.* (ed.). *Millennial Harbinger.* Bethany, Va., and Bethany, W. Va., 1830-70.

Scott, Walter (ed.). *Evangelist.* Cincinnati and Carthage, Ohio, 1832-35; 1838-44.

Winebrenner, John. *History of All Religious Denominations,* chapter on "History of the Disciples of Christ."

VII. *UNPUBLISHED MANUSCRIPTS AND PAPERS*

Arthur, F. P. "The Life of Robert Richardson." Brief manuscript in possession of Mrs. R. H. Wynne, Pittsburgh, Pa.

Chapline, Mary Richardson. "Father's Likes and Dislikes," in "The Life of Dr. Robert Richardson," manuscript by Cloyd Goodnight. Bethany College Library, Bethany, W. Va.

Fall, Philip S. Correspondence. Library of First Christian Church, Frankfort, Ky.

Goodnight, Cloyd. "The Life of Dr. Robert Richardson." Unfinished manuscript, containing a transcript of Richardson's private papers from the Fannie R. Thompson collection. Bethany College Library, Bethany, W. Va.

Minutes of the Board of Trustees of Bethany College. President's office, Bethany, W. Va.

Minutes of the Board of Curators of Kentucky University. Library of the College of the Bible, Lexington, Ky.

Pendleton, A. C. ("Cammie"). Collection of W. K. Pendleton letters. President's office, Bethany College, Bethany, W. Va.

Records of the Carthage Christian church. Library of the College of the Bible, Lexington, Ky.

Richardson, Robert. "Brief History of the Origin and Progress of the Church of Christ at Wellsburg, Brooke Co., Va." Church records, Wellsburg Christian church, Wellsburg, W. Va.

———. Daybook. Lost from Cloyd Goodnight's effects.

———. Personal notebook. Bethany College Library, Bethany, W. Va.

Thompson, Fannie Richardson. Collection of her father's papers, journals, and letters. Copied entire by Cloyd Goodnight from originals, now lost.

Wharton, Emma Richardson. "Father's Last Days," in "The Life of Dr. Robert Richardson," manuscript by Cloyd Goodnight. Bethany College Library, Bethany, W. Va.

INDEX

A

Alexander Campbell, by B. L. Smith, Notes, VI:9, IX:15

"All-sufficiency of Christ," 59

"Alma Mater" (Bethany College song), 199f.

American Agriculturist, 147

American Bible Union, 160f.

American Christian Missionary Society, 142f., 229f.

American Christian Review, 6, 175

American Farmer, 147

American Revision Committee, 160f.

"Ancient Gospel," 45, 48, 58

"Ancient Order," 45

Apostolic Advocate, 78

Apostolic Times, 224

"Atmosphere, The," 143

B

Bacon College, 98, 103, 143, 189

Baconian method, 97

Bakewell, Edwin W., 101

Bakewell, H. N., 62

Baptism, 48, 153, 206. *See also* Immersion

Baptists, 45, 117

"Baptists Against Themselves," 117

Baptists and Disciples, union of, 215f.

Barclay, Decima C. (daughter of A. Campbell) 217f.

Bates, Daniel, 177

Bedford, Nathaniel, 39

Bentley, Adamson, 98, 150

Bethany church, 131, 163, 164, 215, 235

Bethany College, 6, 96, 97-102, 107f., 109-16, 127f., 133f., 136, 137, 143f., 148, 150f., 168, 173, 186f., 190-92, 193, 194-96, 199, 202, 203, 209f., 214f., 217, 219, 225; building destroyed by fire, 186; by-laws of, 101f., 103ff.; chapel of, 132f.; charter of, 98f.; curriculum of, 99, 100f., 115, 131f.; faculty of, 112-16, 214; faculty salaries of, 105, 132, 215; finances of, 99, 100f., 109; museum of, 110; new building of, 194f.; seal of, 111; student enrollment of, 105f., 109f.

Bethany, (W.) Va., 24, 52, 71-73, 75f., 83, 85, 87, 112, 127f., 188, 216, 220, 235

Bethany College Catalogue, Notes, IX:7

Bethany Years, by Woolery, Notes, VIII:1, 3, 9, 10, 11, 15, XI:3, XIII:2, 5, XIV:11, XVII:3

Bethphage, 5, 8, 90f., 94-96, 108, 124f., 128, 132, 136, 145, 146, 147, 161, 163, 188, 196, 201, 207, 213, 218, 224, 231 235f.

Bible, 97, 118, 138-41, 153, 160f., 172

Biblical interpretation: *See* Scripture, interpretation of

Biographical and Historical Catalogue of Washington and Jefferson College, Notes, XIV:13

Black, John, 35f.

Bowman, John B., 189, 191, 194, 196

Boynton, H. B., 144

247